THE
AMERICAN
REVOLUTION
RECONSIDERED

BOOKS BY *Richard B. Morris*

The American Revolution Reconsidered (*1967*)

The Peacemakers (*1965*)

Great Presidential Decisions (*1960*)

The Spirit of 'Seventy-Six (WITH HENRY STEELE COMMAGER, *1958, 1967*)

Alexander Hamilton and the Founding of the Nation (*1957*)

The American Revolution: A Brief History (*1955*)

Encyclopedia of American History (FIRST EDITION, *1953*)

Fair Trial (*1953*)

A Treasury of Great Reporting (WITH LOUIS L. SNYDER, *1949*)

Government and Labor in Early America (*1946*)

The Era of the American Revolution (EDITOR, *1939*)

Studies in the History of American Law (*1930*)

A Guide to the Principal Sources for Early American History (WITH EVARTS BOUTELL GREENE, *1929*)

Volumes I and II of

The LIFE History of the United States:

The New World (*1963*)

The Making of the Nation (*1963*)

THE
AMERICAN
REVOLUTION
RECONSIDERED

Richard B. Morris

HARPER & ROW, PUBLISHERS

NEW YORK, EVANSTON, AND LONDON

TO *JEFFREY*

Contents

Preface

"Was there ever a revolution brought about, especially so important as this, without great internal tumults and violent convulsions!" Samuel Adams asked rhetorically. Himself a catalyst to those same revolutionary forces, Adams could not have phrased a question more apt or one more pertinent either for his or our time. It seems as much a miracle to us as it did to Adams' generation that the American Revolution managed to achieve decolonization, nationhood, constitutional reform, and even a measure of social and economic change without enkindling class war or suffering violent reaction.

The approach of the bicentennial commemorating the American Revolution suggests an occasion if not a need to re-examine that epoch. Each generation re-writes its past, and ours has proved no exception. Recent writers have depicted the American Revolution as a conservative movement, essentially political in its objectives, embraced by a people who had already achieved an egalitarian society. So restricted a conception of the American Revolution constitutes an enormous oversimplification, and as such should not be permitted to stand uncorrected.

If the Revolution was just a War for Independence, if the conflicts which came in its wake did not transcend what Jefferson called a "contest of principle between the advocates of republicanism and those of kingly government," it would have little meaning for the Nuclear Space Age. We are not concerned today with the menace of kingly governments, but we are still capable of being aroused by forces that pose a threat to freedom. We still share the conviction of the Revolutionary generation that governments should rest upon the consent of the governed, that the rights of minorities should be respected, and we are still moved to action by exploitation, injustice, poverty, and ignorance. To that radically reshaped world in which we live, the message of the American Revolution is as relevant as its meaning is profound.

In quite a different sense, too, the American Revolution needs to be re-studied. American governments, past as well as present, have been habitually criticized abroad, perhaps unfairly at times, for imposing their preferences as to governmental systems upon other peoples, and for assuming that America is not only the arsenal of democracy but the chosen guardian of moral values. What disturbs even some of our friends is our posture of being not only right but righteous as well. If this is the way we have become it is also the way we have acted from the very beginning. From its inception the American Revolution was pitched on a moral plane. The Patriots were concerned not only about mankind's good opinion, but, as Tom Paine felicitously phrased it, believed it to be in their power "to make a world happy." If the Americans had only been a little more parochial about their Revolution they might have turned into a more introverted people, and American history, and that of the world, would have taken so different a turning. That Americans now venture to shoulder global responsibilities of awesome dimension is in no small part the result of their rearing during the infancy of this republic.

The assumption of world responsibility demands a good deal of intellectual flexibility. What Americans took from their Revolution, above all, was a tolerance of change, an ingredient which, it need scarcely be pointed out, is as indispensable in any approach to contemporary problems posed by the underdeveloped nations as it was in reshaping our own world back in 1776.

These four essays directed to a reconsideration of the American Revolution formed the substance of a series of public lectures delivered in 1966 at New York University under the Anson G. Phelps Lectureship on Early American History. Since then they have been substantially expanded, and portions of two of the essays which had appeared in the *William and Mary Quarterly* have been extensively revised.

RICHARD B. MORRIS

THE
AMERICAN
REVOLUTION
RECONSIDERED

I

THE HISTORIANS
AND THE
AMERICAN
REVOLUTION

The American Revolution inaugurated an epoch of un-usual complexity and vast magnitude. The embittered Massachusetts Tory, Peter Oliver, likened its coming to volcanic action, and even at this remote distance the metaphor seems fitting. Like a volcanic eruption the Revolution's rumblings and seismic manifestations might have been picked up long in advance by those trained to observe and reflect, and like a gigantic volcanic disturb-ance it spewed forth its hot lava great distances from the crater. Its shocks can be felt to the present day, and its ashes have been spread by the winds to the four quarters of the world. It may have started at Lexington, but it continues in Birmingham, and Saigon, and Lagos.

/ 1

Historians both of the Left and of the Right have subjected the Age of Revolutions to extensive revision, while professional revolutionaries find their model in the French rather than the American Revolution, drawing inspiration not only from the upheaval which toppled Louis XVI from his throne but more immediately from the Communard uprising of 1871 and its terrible suppression. Latin Americanists tell us that the American Revolution, as a successful challenge to the Old Order, affected the minds of men in the rest of the Americas, but that the French Revolution in its Napoleonic expression more immediately touched off that long struggle between *creoles* and *peninsulares* which freed Latin America from Spanish and Portuguese rule.[1]*

Obsessed with the modern image of revolutions as possessing a proletarian character, some critics like Hannah Arendt would have us believe that the French Revolution, which ended in disaster, "has made world history," however imprecise the phrase, while the triumphantly successful American Revolution "has remained an event of little more than local importance."[2] With better balance, a recent scholar has persuasively argued the thesis that the American was part of "one big revolutionary agitation" which spread throughout the Western world.[3] Discounting the minuscule revolutionary upthrust in the tiny republic of Geneva in the 1760's and the heroic effort of little Corsica to free herself of colonialism a few years later, there is no gainsaying the fact that it was the American Revolution that set off the chain reaction. Nor can one afford to ignore the prototype role of the American Revolution as the first example in modern history of a successful revolt against the Established Order. That it also provided the first lessons in how to achieve decolonization and how to move forward from colonial subordina-

* A section of numbered notes appears at the end of each chapter.

tion to equality among states gives it a peculiar pertinence to our own day.

Perhaps at no time in the twentieth century since the Russian Revolution have people been as conscious of the winds of change as today. That we are living in another revolutionary epoch, in many ways more revolutionary than any that have gone before, is a self-evident proposition. We have managed to accommodate ourselves to a Keynesian Revolution and to seeing the notion of a welfare state now universally accepted. We are in the process also of digesting a Nuclear Space Revolution, a revolution in communications technology, a population explosion, a civil rights revolution, a revolution in family and sexual mores, a disintegration of deference, and radical departures from accepted norms in the cultural disciplines, along with a series of political revolutions in islands close by and lands most distant. These last have not only tipped the balance of power against the old European states and divided the world into two, perhaps even three, areas of ideological and military tension but they have touched off a whole series of nationalist movements which have freed almost the entire colonial world from its traditional European masters. It is this facet of our present neo-Revolutionary Era which poses the most tantalizing analogies to the American Revolution.

Primarily, though by no means exclusively, the American Revolution must be considered as an anticolonial war for independence, the first of many to follow. It takes on an extra dimension, however, by being not only a war of liberation from overseas rule but a war for freedom; by its insistent quest not only for independence but for the achievement of constitutional guarantees incompatible with its erstwhile colonial status.

There are those who regard the present world posture of the United States as inconsistent with its revolutionary past. These critics, both at home and abroad, feel that this nation is now obsessed with its central role as guarantor of world stability. Viewing the current unrest in the underdeveloped areas as a residue of our own revolutionary tradition, they regard the so-called "wars of national liberation" as designed to end colonialism, which has now become a pejorative word. Hence, they would depict America as the leader of a new Holy Alliance set up to maintain legitimacy and the *status quo*. The facts that these "wars of national liberation" are not infrequently thinly disguised wars of aggression and that the United States in opposing them seeks "freedom" for the victims of terror and force rather than the establishment of a neo-colonial status in which America merely assumes the role of the Old World powers that have abdicated their authority may appear to be self-evident propositions to those who seek to halt Communist aggression. Unhappily, neither our avowed enemies nor even our more friendly critics are prepared to accept these propositions. Although we are reaching for the stars and have showered less favored peoples with our benevolence in unmatched flow, our motives are profoundly misunderstood and our military intentions widely distrusted.

On one other occasion in American history has this nation's revolutionary past been exploited by its critics to confuse and weaken the national will. The American Civil War posed a dilemma in a way comparable with that of the present. Then one side was fighting for self-determination and the other for freedom, twin objectives of the American Revolution. Both sides appealed to the Spirit of '76, thereby revealing an enormous cleavage in the way each interpreted the meaning of the American Revolution. Those who found in the Revolution support for the doctrine of state sovereignty were confronted with the countervailing argument that the Revolution was an expression of national will and a first move toward national unity, and that of all the pieces in the fabric that makes up our revolutionary past freedom was the most vibrant. Admittedly, the phrase "all men are created equal" did not accurately depict the America of 1776, wherein almost a half million persons were held in bondage. But as Abraham Lincoln saw it on the eve of the Civil War, in speaking of the Great Declaration and the men of Jefferson's generation, "They meant to set up a standard maxim for a free society, which should be . . . constantly looked to, constantly labored for, and even though never perfectly attained, constantly approximated, and thereby constantly spreading and deepening its influence and augmenting the happiness and value of life to all people of all colors everywhere." Confronted with the greatest crisis in our nation's history, Lincoln prudently defined the right of revolution enunciated in the Declaration of Independence as "a moral right," which could be exercised only for overriding moral causes.[4]

If the objectives of the American Revolution were pertinent to the ends for which the Civil War was waged, an equal if not stronger case can be made for demonstrating the relevance of the Great Declaration to the issues of our own day. Intellectuals have systematically dismantled most of the underpinnings of the Declaration. Santayana termed it "a salad of illusions," combining "admiration for the noble savage, for the ancient Romans (whose republic was founded on slavery and war) mixed with the quietistic maxims of the Sermon on the Mount."[5] Modern critics have taken relish in demonstrating that the Declaration was founded on weak history and a naïve faith in progress and human perfectibility shared by the prophets of the Enlightenment. Notwithstanding its detractors, this humane literary utterance has demonstrated exceptionally durable qualities and still conveys a meaningful message to a world where authoritarian traditions remain deeply rooted and where materialism and pessimism have largely

supplanted ethical values set in a rational and even opti-
mistic framework. It is paradoxical that almost all nations
pay glib tribute to the unalienable rights of man for
which the Revolution was ostensibly fought as well as to
the concept of government by consent of the governed,
even lands where freedom and democracy are conspicuous by their systematic suppression.

The race question has once more propelled the Declaration to the forefront of political charters. When the Prime
Minister of Rhodesia can piously affirm that his nation,
which denies equal rights to a majority of its inhabitants,
is steadfast to the principles of the American Revolution,
it seems patent that his constricted conception of that
great event accords with neither the facts nor the view
about them generally held by Americans today. Indeed, at
no time since September of 1783, when the peacemakers
affixed their signatures to the Definitive Treaty at the
Hotel d'York in Paris, have there been more compelling
reasons than the present for us to reconsider our revolution and review our judgments about our revolutionary
era. As is true with all judgments about the past, these
may still be tentative, partial, and colored by present
interests and perils,[6] but we now possess so vast a fund of
evidence about the American Revolution that we have no
grounds for putting such judgments off to some indefinite
future time.

The older historical writers who molded the form in
which our eighteenth-century past has been frozen, along
with the textbook writers who slavishly and unimagina-
tively copied the model, must bear a good deal of the
responsibility for the unrealistic conception of the American Revolution held by so many Americans. If the
teacher's re-creation of the distant past is too often no
more successful than the pomp and pageantry of a cos-
tume movie depicting the era of the Revolution, it is
because our look at the past has so often lacked both

depth and imagination. Too many people think of the American Revolution as exemplified by a statuesque and easily recognizable Founding Father standing up in an open boat, which rowers are desperately maneuvering through the ice-choked Delaware. If the past of knee breeches, tricornered hats, and powdered wigs is frozen on Leutze's famous canvas it has been solidified in marble and bronze in countless statues in which the great Patriots are made to take heroic poses. Somehow the Founding Fathers do not come through to our present world, to the jet set, the civil rights demonstrators, the workers on a Ford assembly line, the antidraft protesters, or even to the children of this TV age, who still have the capacity for imaginative projection and to whom pageantry has more than the hollow externals it presents to sophisticated adults.

It is easy to allocate the blame to good Parson Weems and to the Fourth of July oratory which carried on his tradition of depicting the leadership as omniscient and all-virtuous, while continuing to portray Washington and his associates as monuments rather than men. The good Parson, a backwoods huckster who, with his perfervid rhetoric would have been a sensation on Madison Avenue today, made Washington into the sanctimonious marble image that he remains for most Americans despite the valiant efforts of Paul Leicester Ford, Rupert Hughes, Douglas Southall Freeman, and, most recently, James T. Flexner.

On a more serious level of scholarship than the Parson, Jared Sparks deliberately prettied up the writings of Washington. He would not even allow the forthright and occasionally explosive Patriot such harmless phrases as "not amount to a flea bite," censored the verb "prostitute," altered other references on religion and God, and performed comparable emasculations of the prose of Franklin and Gouverneur Morris, two very salty personalities.

Since Sparks was a respectable scholar, indeed one might say that as President of Harvard College he was a member of the Establishment, few had the temerity to question his inaccuracies and distortions, and, as shall be shown, his tamperings with the diplomatic sources of the Revolution contributed to the creation of that classic image of a disinterested France coming to the aid of American liberty, an image as lacking in sophistication as it was in shadings, but one most Americans dearly cherished down to the Era of *le Général*.

Unhappily, the detractors, muckrakers, and so-called realists of the twentieth century have, by seeking to redress the balance, only managed to highlight the trivia, the spurious, and the meretricious while too often losing sight of the depth, subtlety, and complexity of American Revolutionary personalities. If they have made the Founding Fathers more human, they have also managed to portray them as implausibly petty. How much idle speculation has been wasted over whether George Washington did or did not have an affair with Sally Fairfax? How little on what made a man of Washington's background a radical? A recent writer has engrossed himself in research and come up with the discovery that Benjamin Franklin fancied himself as something of a philanderer. It would be far more to the point if he could have shed light on the innumerable paradoxes that Franklin's career represents. Was Franklin the "kindly old Ben" his admirers envisage, or the "cunning opportunist" he appears to his critics? A man of humble origins, he cultivated the powerful and the rich, and walked out on the common-law wife of whom he never could be proud. A prince of pragmatists with an eye to the main chance, he preached good works and strict morality; but he, his son, and his grandson all fathered illegitimate offspring. Noted for his candor, he had a curious talent for deception, and perpetrated a steady stream of literary hoaxes. Although Max Weber persisted in presenting Franklin as a true Calvinist in his admiration of labor for labor's sake, the good Doctor, while exhorting others to work, was himself no lover of toil. In the great confrontations between Franklin and John Adams in Paris, during the years of tedious diplomatic negotiation that brought the Revolution to a close, it was the "old conjurer's" long spells of apathy, along with his saltiness and his studied reticences, that both baffled and infuriated his irrepressible and quarrelsome associate. If Franklin seemed lazy, he had an intellectual curiosity that bespoke an alert and wide-ranging intellect. If he had an eye for the main chance, he also had an extraordinarily selfless interest in popular education and the wide spectrum of humanitarian efforts. Thus, the Sage of Passy succeeded in baffling his contemporaries, and he has eluded most scholars since then.

Hidden depths, complexity, a talent for rationalizing public interest and private motive, along with strength of purpose and a sense of dedication constitute some of the keys to the characters of the men who took this nation to the brink of Revolution, then successfully guided the craft over the cataract to a safe haven. Take our good friend John Adams, the Braintree lawyer. Adjectives like testy, quarrelsome, forthright are customarily used to explain the functioning of this prickly but marvelously alive and unusually complex human being. The publication of the diary, autobiography, family and legal papers of John Adams provides insights into Adams' character and motivations hitherto unsuspected. No one has ventured to challenge the courage of John Adams in undertaking the unpopular defense of Captain Preston and the British Redcoats in the so-called Boston Massacre trials. That is part of the mythology of the Revolution. More than three decades later Adams recorded that, when asked to assume the defense of Captain Preston, he answered unhesitatingly, "Counsel ought to be the very last thing that an accused person should want in a free country." That is the tradition, but new facts about the conduct of the defense disclosed by the *Adams Legal Papers* suggest that the actual role of the Patriot defense attorneys, John Adams and his associate Josiah Quincy, Jr., was more subtle and less forthright than Adams' reputed remarks on accepting the defense role would indicate.

First of all, despite the efforts of Samuel Adams and other hotheads to press for an immediate trial, John Adams, of counsel for the defense, doubtless in cahoots with the Tory-minded Lieutenant Governor, saw to it that the trial was postponed until some of the excitement had died down. Secondly, the defense made the crucial but sensible decision to sever the trials in order to avoid the risk of mass convictions. Captain Preston was tried first. His acquittal made the rest anticlimactic. It may destroy some illusions, but the evidence now in shows that the jury was packed, that five of the twelve were later Loyalist exiles and were doing business with the British army well before the trial. Surely Adams knew this, if he had not connived at it. More startling, perhaps, is the revelation of Adams' conduct on cross-examination. Hero or no, in going to the defense of the hated British officer, Adams prudently toned down the slashing cross-examination that his co-counsel had planned because he did not want the conduct of the town of Boston to be blackened. As a Patriot he was not anxious to bring out on cross-examination evidence showing that the expulsion of the British troops from the town of Boston was a plan concocted by the townspeople.

True, Adams was confident that he had evidence enough without it for acquittal, but his relatively gentle treatment of Crown witnesses raises a nice ethical question. How far should a lawyer permit his political ties to influence his judgment of the most effective means of conducting a trial in his client's interest? In this case

Adams enjoyed the best of two worlds. He added luster to his rising reputation by securing his client's acquittal, but he prudently avoided damaging his standing as a Patriot. Had the case gone the other way, Adams might have been justifiably the subject of serious censure.

Now, we have here all the elements of a tense, unpredictable trial drama, rather than a patriotic morality play depicting virtue against sin. Just because the protagonists of the American Revolution cannot be authentically demonstrated to have been all black or all white does not make them neutral gray. Still the neutralists who stood as long as they could in the middle ground provide some extraordinary revelations into character and motivation while affording us a specially close view of the stern civil war that was waged in America. Consider the case of the New York jurist and historian, William Smith, a leading lawyer, whose *Historical Memoirs* reveal his intimate connection with the Sons of Liberty. An imperialist rather than a nationalist, Smith refused to take the fateful step of forswearing allegiance to his King. Yet he was never completely repudiated by the Patriots, never completely accepted by the Tories. Although he was in effect confined for his suspected loyalism, the committee of the New York Provincial Convention freely consulted him in drafting New York's notable Constitution of 1777. Finally banished by the Committee for Detecting and Defeating Conspiracies, he became a leading civilian official in New York City under British rule. Although nominally the British chief justice, he tipped off Patriot Governor Clinton of Ethan Allen's dubious dealings with General Carleton, thereby leaking top secrets from British headquarters. In doing so, he acted as a stakeholder in the New Yorkers' claims to Vermont lands. Should New York maintain its title to Vermont lands, a title which could have been confirmed by a British victory, he would have been personally far better off then had Vermont, by seceding from the Thirteen rebellious Colonies succeeded in winning its title fight. For his inconstant loyalty Smith was to be rewarded by his King by being made chief justice of Canada.

Smith doubtless rationalized his behavior, but it is dubious whether some of the more notorious double-dealers suffered qualms of conscience, men like Benjamin Thompson, for example. One of the very few eminent men of science to have been a native of the American colonies, Thompson was, in addition, a turncoat and a spy, a man who readily deserted both wife and country without apparent remorse. Yet his shallow egoism was tempered by a broad streak of humanitarian concern, and he applied his scientific knowledge to social ends. He sent important military information about the Patriot militia to British Army headquarters, and sought at the same time to sell epaulets to the American forces. In England his attachment to Lord George Germain's family set tongues wagging, and it was rumored and continued to be rumored that he had been engaged in espionage, in leaking secrets from the British Admiralty to France and Spain, nations then at war with England. He had all the qualities of audacity, impudence, and amorality to qualify for a counterspy, but at the same time he possessed a restless curiosity that set him above the drab level of international rogues and impelled him to devise scientific improvements and social reforms, ranging from kitchen ranges, roasters, parlor grates, and fireplaces to workhouses and soup kitchens. A great eccentric, who, following his own scientific principles, dressed in white from head to foot and rode in a carriage with very wide wheel rims, this strangely talented but twisted man has still managed to keep his biographers from penetrating the wall which he successfully built around himself.

Or consider the curious case of Dr. Edward Bancroft. For a long time innuendoes were spread about Bancroft, innuendoes dating from his role in the American Revolution. Almost a century later Francis Wharton, the respected editor of the diplomatic papers of the Revolution, went out of his way to brand as false the rumors that the Doctor was both a traitor and a spy. Unfortunately for both the Doctor and the learned editor, subsequently uncovered British documents proved Wharton wrong on both counts. What makes a scoundrel like Bancroft multidimensional, however, was his honest concern for the good opinion of men like Franklin and Jay whom he admired and systematically deceived. Indubitably, he corrupted Silas Deane, a Patriot whose early contributions to the Revolution in securing Franco-Spanish assistance proved of considerable magnitude. Yet Deane was completely insensitive to the notion of conflict of interest that some, certainly not all, Patriots recognized. Blind to his own weaknesses of character, convinced of his nation's ingratitude, Deane easily persuaded himself that it was in America's true interest to end the conflict and remain within the British Empire. If he became an avowed defector from the American cause, he did so at a price. Men like Bancroft and Deane were complex men. They were devious men. They walked the treacherous path of divided loyalties in an era when the concept of national allegiance was less rigid than in our own time. Even at this remote distance it is fascinating to observe their intrigues and maneuvers and to speculate on their motivations.

If some of the American personages involved in the Revolutionary struggle afford examples of complex motivations, the British leaders during that crisis pose a challenge of at least equal dimension to biographer or analyst. Many factors indubitably entered into their decision making, but surely their personal problems cannot be ruled out. Reviewing their peculiar behavior as statesmen under pressure, we must constantly bear in mind that Charles

Townshend had suffered under a domineering father, that the devious and secretive Lord Shelburne acknowledged that he had been unloved in childhood, and that Sir Henry Clinton, touchy, opinionated, suspicious, suffered his basic insecurity to rot out the core of his generalship, with the result that he observed from afar the catastrophe at Yorktown in a state of shock. A clue to the obstinacy and obsessive meddlesomeness of George III is suggested by his loathing for his wife and his state of constant warfare with his children.

If we have lost sight of the people who waged the war, it is partly the fault of the pompous or trivial portraits of the leadership with which biographers have beguiled us, but it is also the responsibility of some twentieth-century historians who would bury the American Revolution in the Procrustean bed of a determinism of one sort or another, leaving little or no room for freedom of choice and virtually none for the role of the individual in decision making. If the individual is the product of his time, he is not necessarily the helpless pawn of movements or forces. If he is not master of his own destiny, he still plays a large and responsible role in shaping it.

Aside from the failure to probe people as well as causes deeply and insightfully, historians have contributed to the confusion over the nature of the American Revolution by failing to agree on the most elementary matter of determining when it began. Both the Patriots and the Loyalists, it must be conceded, laid the foundations for the historians' confusion. The articulate John Adams, who still manages to be both quoted and quotable on both sides of a number of issues, once said, many years after the event, that the Revolution was "in the minds of the people, and this was effected, from 1760 to 1775, in the course of fifteen years before a drop of blood was drawn at Lexington."[7] Of course, Adams did not mean this literally, any more than Jefferson did when he advocated a revolution every twenty years. Indeed, some contemporaries would not have agreed with Adams as to when the Revolution began, and others, like Benjamin Rush, would not have subscribed to his view as to when it ended.

If one conceives of the Revolution as a movement of political nationalism, culminating in a secession from empire, there is much to support Adams' view. Aside from the new imperial decisions after 1763 which stirred up colonial resistance, the fifteen years before the Revolution are years of extraordinary growth and maturity. Between 1750 and 1776 the population of the American colonies almost doubled, in part the result of exceptionally heavy immigration continuing to the very start of the conflict. By 1776 the entire coastal enclave from Maine to Georgia was settled, and the trans-Appalachian frontier probed. Extraordinary gains had been made in the volume of agricultural staples exported, mercantile firms flourished as never before, and urban affluence, along with some upstart poverty, laid the foundations for elegant living for a business élite as well as a planter élite, not to speak of a political élite enjoying a considerable measure of self-rule. Demographic and economic growth went hand in hand with a sense of cultural difference from the mother country, with a feeling of self-sufficiency indubitably fed by the results of the Seven Years' War, which eliminated the traditional French enemy from the North American continent.[8]

Englishmen did not view as unmixed blessings the affluence and expansion of America, along with its tradition of nonconformity. As early as 1745 Malachy Postlethwayt opposed furnishing the colonies with white labor from either the mother country or the Continent on the ground that such emigration would serve to make the colonies manufacturing rivals of England. Let them stick to slaves, he argued. That would tend to keep the colonies agricultural.[9] Major General Thomas Gage, who commanded the British armies in North America, wrote his superior in 1768:

> I have never heard of a people . . . who could manufacture without hands, or materials. We read also that many manufacturers embark for America but can't discover where they land. . . . It would be well, if the emigrations from Great Britain, Ireland and Holland, where the Germans embark for America, were prevented; and our new settlements should be peopled from the old ones, which would be a means to thin them, and put it less in their power to do mischief.[10]

In short, the rapid maturation of the American colonies in the generation ending with revolution served as a seedbed for notions of nationalism and independence while consciously shaping the new guidelines which the British ministry sought to put into effect, and with such fateful consequences.

Since the colonies had been nurtured in a dissenting tradition, had from the start enjoyed a considerable measure of independence, and had come in fact to view themselves as virtually self-governing entities, one might well argue that the Revolution began when the first Englishmen came to Jamestown and Plymouth. A respectable company of Tory historians took that view, insisting that almost from the first landings the colonists had aimed at independence. So argued Samuel Seabury, who accused New England of having deliberately provoked a crisis in order to force the other colonies to join in her predetermined drive for independence. Joseph Galloway and George Chalmers made the same point,[11] and it was pressed home far less temperately by Peter Oliver, the disillusioned Tory chief justice of Massachusetts. The latter, it must be said, differentiated between what he called "the long-term causes of rebellion," in which category he included religious separatism and the revolution of 1689 in Massachusetts, from the "immediate causes," uppermost being the failure of Governor Bernard to appoint James Otis senior to the chief justiceship of the province. As Oliver saw it, the result of the elder Otis' being passed over sparked the formation of a faction supporting the junior Otis, and including "the black regiment," leading figures in the Puritan clergy—all joined in systematic opposition to the new chief justice, Thomas Hutchinson. That worthy happened also to double as lieutenant governor, and through intermarriage with the Olivers controlled a scandalous number of royal offices.

Oliver's view of the immediate causes of the Revolution varies in detail but hardly in substance from the classic Whig account. It was John Adams who, describing James Otis' memorable arguments in the Writs of Assistance Case, arguments made even more memorable in the retelling, remarked retrospectively, "Then and there the Child Independence was born." Indeed, a most recent historian of the British Empire, Lawrence H. Gipson, puts the Loyalist case pithily in a chapter titled "Massachusetts Foments Rebellion."[12] Even the Patriot historian David Ramsay implies that prior to 1774 the other colonies "were happy, and had no cause, on their own account, to oppose the government, Great Britain."[13]

The trouble with these judgments, as regards both the remote and the immediate causes of the revolt, is that, even granted their premises, they put the Revolution down to a New England conspiracy, begun when flint-faced Governor Endecott cut the cross out of the English flag in Salem back in the early 1630's, and revitalized one hundred and thirty years later by the anti-Hutchinson cabal. But Massachusetts did not fight alone. Twelve other colonies joined her, and there is no proof that they were simply the puppets of Otis, that "Jack Cade of the Rebellion," as Peter Oliver regarded him, and by Otis' successors in the radical leadership of the Bay Colony.

Granted that Massachusetts was politically the most mature of the colonies; granted, too, that she nursed serious grievances, it must be recognized that the other mainland colonies had long since cast off their swaddling clothes and were also laboring under grievances, often quite different from those that kept wounds festering in New England.

Virginia, a leading debtor colony, suffered acutely from the currency stringency, which the British government, by disallowing the Twopenny Act, failed to alleviate. It is somehow significant that virtually every Virginia planter became a Patriot and every single Virginia merchant became a Tory. Patrick Henry's passionate defense of the vestry against the Rev. James Maury's lawsuit for back wages owing him—in fact for three times as much money as the Twopenny Act allotted him—is as much a part of the mythology of the Revolution as James Otis' argument against the Writs of Assistance. It was Henry who declared, according to Maury's own contemporary account, that "a king who annuls or disallows laws of so salutary a nature, from being the father of his people degenerates into a tyrant and forfeits all rights to obedience." It was on that occasion that the opposing counsel cried out "Treason!" and the Royalists among the spectators took up the cry. So early did Patrick Henry press his attack on monarchical power, employing language that anticipated by a few years his heated remarks, varyingly reported, made in the course of the debates on the Stamp Act Resolves.

Deep and varied grievances stirred discontent in the Thirteen Colonies and ultimately inspired common action. For example, New York, the original headquarters of the British command, had long nursed irritations over troop quartering. Merchant tycoons like Henry Laurens in Charleston, John Hancock in Boston, and the Browns of Providence all bore visible bruises from contact with a severe, mayhap harsh, customs enforcement machinery. Each in turn was inspired to bestir himself about it. The course of the Browns in plotting the burning of the revenue cutter *Gaspee* in Rhode Island waters was both violent and lawless, but it is significant that when the British government took steps to investigate that scandalous act of defiance, it was the House of Burgesses in Virginia, a body of men representing a constituency least concerned with problems of smuggling, which reacted promptly by instigating the colonial committees of correspondence. That indispensable link joined together the chain of concerted action by which the Thirteen Colonies were to achieve independence.

There is still another and even more persuasive argument against putting the American Revolution down to a New England cabal. To do so implies that the colonists were aggressively seeking to sever their links to the Crown, but prior to 1775 there is a complete absence of evidence to support this view. Rather than making alleged colonial conspirators the villains of the piece, one has enough evidence at hand to build a strong case against British officialdom. It was that new conception of the British Empire, initiated at Whitehall, and holding out the clear prospect of curtailing America's constitutional liberties, that in effect touched off the series of crises. Most recently, in their fragmented biography of Charles Townshend, Sir Lewis Namier and John Brooke disclose that it was Townshend who, as a junior minister back in August, 1753, drafted instructions for Sir Danvers Osborn, Governor of New York, which Horace Walpole caustically described as "better calculated for the latitude of Mexico and for a Spanish tribunal, than for a free, rich British settlement."[14] These instructions charged the New York Assembly with trampling upon the royal authority and prerogative by assuming "to themselves the disposal of public money"; directed it to make permanent provision for the salaries of the governor, judges, and other officials and for the security of the province and any foreseeable charges. The money was to be applied by warrants from the Governor advised by the Council, the Assembly being merely permitted "from time to time to view and examine . . . accounts." If carried out, Townshend's instructions would have rendered the royal executive financially independent of the colonial assembly. As Namier and Brooke point out, Townshend aimed at a reshaping of colonial government to which the raising of a revenue by act of the British Parliament became a necessary corollary.[15]

It was this same brilliant but frivolous "Champagne Charlie," as his intimates called him, who, in the course of the debates over the Stamp Act, which he supported, asserted the supremacy of the mother country over the colonies, concluding his speech in favor of the Stamp Bill with a peroration which might have been drawn from one of his own father's letters to him:

> And now will these Americans, children planted by our care, nourished up by our indulgence until they are grown to a degree of strength and opulence, and protected by our arms, will they grudge to contribute their mite to relieve us from the heavy weight of that burden which we lie under?

In reply Colonel Isaac Barré delivered his celebrated indictment of the mother country: "They planted by your care? No! Your oppressions planted them in America. . . . They nourished by your indulgence? They grew by your neglect of them."[16]

Perhaps we need not subscribe to Namier and Brooke's heavyhanded psychology in assuming that Townshend, who had suffered as the oppressed son, now became toward the colonies the heavy father. Nevertheless, it is clear that Townshend's program embraced not only devices to raise a revenue from America by his ill-fated

Townshend Acts, but also to reduce the extent of colonial self-government and to reassert British authority.

At a time when, as Chancellor of the Exchequer and member of the Cabinet, Townshend was still politically concerned with the affairs of the East India Company, he speculated in the Company's stock, purchasing shares in the names of other men and selling them at a neat profit made possible in large part by his inside information and public remarks. It is this gay and thoroughly amoral political figure who managed to pledge the Cabinet to a tax policy they disapproved, a tax he himself worked out, and which he had pledged to raise a month before the government had been defeated in its attempt to keep the Land Tax from being reduced. The one had nothing to do with the other. The revenue raised by the Townshend duties was in any case to be used entirely in America, and was, furthermore, too small to cover the loss of revenue suffered by the reduction of the Land Tax. Indeed, Townshend's plan was not merely a fiscal measure but part of a grand design to strengthen British authority in the colonies, and to make the royal officials independent of the colonial assemblies, a design which he had disclosed back in 1753. It was patently aimed at depriving the colonies of what they had come to regard as their constitutional liberties, the control of the purse by their elected legislatures. If there was a plot, then, it was not concocted by Otis or Adams but was the brain child of Charles Townshend, and the Townshend Acts of 1767 were the capstone on the schemes launched fourteen years earlier by a very junior minister who had already begun to articulate a bold plan to bring America into due subordination.[17]

Much has been written recently to demonstrate the connection between our recent pre-Vietnam conservative cast of thought and contemporary writing about the American Revolution, which, it is charged, reflects this new conservatism, and even constitutes a Back-to-Bancroft movement, although George Bancroft, by the standards of his day, was hardly a conservative. It has been argued that our affluent society tends to blur differences and sees the American past in its more homogenized aspect.[18] The criticism is meant perhaps neither as a compliment to George Bancroft, the ablest representative of the second generation of historians of the American Revolution, nor to some of the contemporary writers whose sophisticated formulations have been conveniently oversimplified.

True, there has been a flight from the rather rigid and artificially applied determinism of the Populist-Progressive historians, and in America, if not in England, the neo-Whigs are in the saddle. But is theirs the same revolution that the first Whig historians and then Bancroft painted with bold strokes on a broad canvas?

That first generation of Whig historians, themselves eyewitnesses of the Revolution, have come in for a lot of humorless criticism. Historical scholarship was then hardly the sophisticated instrument it has become. Today it often consists of plagiarizing, or at least paraphrasing, from a multitude of sources, the most pertinent ones carefully concealed. In those more naïve days the writers borrowed from a single source and generally made no bones about it. The primary source for their facts was Dodsley's *Annual Register*, a British news summary, which was at least as objective as current news weeklies and surprisingly lively. What illuminated and informed the pages devoted to the American Revolution was the fact that they came from the graceful pen of Edmund Burke. Scrupulous as to dates and facts, Burke could hardly conceal his sympathies for the American cause or his attachment to the Parliamentary Opposition which opposed the conduct of the war.

Of that first generation of historians, William Gordon admitted wholesale borrowings from the *Annual Register*, and so did David Ramsay, a distinct cut above Gordon as historian and interpreter. A Princeton graduate who practiced medicine in Charleston and served in the Continental Congress, Ramsay, though a participant in the great events of the war, writes of them in a curiously detached spirit. He is far less impassioned than the combatants who took up their pens in later generations. Ramsay's facts may not be impeccable, but his judgments are sensible and his evaluation of causation astonishingly profound. He sees the Revolution as more than a response to a catalogue of grievances accumulating shortly before its outbreak (he discounts the alleged hardships suffered by the colonies under the earlier Mercantilist enactments), but recognizes the importance of distance, of the dissenting tradition in religion, of the intellectual currents of the Enlightenment and the English Whig tradition, of the relative degree of social equality prevailing in the colonies, and the long-established constitutional liberties exercised therein, along with the gradual erosion among successive generations of colonists of the bonds of affection for the mother country. In appraising the motivations for revolt, he even gives credit to age and temperament, finding that older Americans were seldom warm Whigs while the younger and more ardent spirits were more readily drawn into the movement.[19] Thus, Ramsay provides us with no convenient whipping boys, neither a malevolent unbalanced George III nor a set of tyrannical ministers. Indeed, as he remarks, the problems were beyond the grasp of ordinary statesmen, "whose minds were narrowed by the formalities of laws or the trammels of office." Franklin, in 1773, put the troubles down to a purblindness of comprehension among the ruling set, a neat clinical analysis to which Ramsay subscribed.

With George Bancroft, foremost among the next generation of writers on the American Revolution, the polemical note becomes more strident. George III, in the perspective of the Whig tradition, takes on an authoritarian character, while the Americans are depicted as pressing along the path of progress according to God's plan. It is democracy. It is manifest destiny. It is even low tariff, which might be expected of a strong Jacksonian Democrat. As an opponent of trade barriers Bancroft gives to the British mercantile program a more important dimension than most earlier writers. Viewing the colonial mercantile systems as the "head-spring which colored all the stream" of independence, he failed to distinguish the Molasses Act of 1733, which, as John Adams pointed out, was systematically flouted through connivance with venal customs officers, and the earlier Navigation Acts, which Lawrence A. Harper has demonstrated to have been rather scrupulously enforced. Finally, in an age when the issue of Union was uppermost, the Constitution to Bancroft becomes the culmination and fulfillment of the Revolution.

Although no man prior to George Bancroft took as much pains as he did to search out and copy pertinent materials from the foreign archives, and no one before or since perhaps has presented as comprehensive a view of the war, he signally and unaccountably failed to utilize much of the documentation that he had gathered, too often substituting purple prose for a reasoned evaluation of the evidence. Thus, after considering the Coercive Acts and the Quebec Act, Bancroft remarked, "In this manner Great Britain, allured by a phantom of absolute authority over colonies, made war on human freedom." In short, to an age which eschews rhetoric, Bancroft at many points appears to have much less to say to us today than his predecessor David Ramsay. Bancroft's romantic nationalism and his devout commitment to progress found expression in John Fiske's literary evocation of the American Revolution. Therein Fiske saw the Revolution as the first step in the forward march of a people whose innate superiority was accepted by him as a vindication of Darwinian principles.

History is never written in a vacuum, and the American Revolution seems particularly responsive to prevailing political and intellectual currents. Shortly after George Bancroft completed his Author's Last Revision, two entirely different approaches to the American Revolutionary Era were in the course of formulation. It was not purely fortuitous that they should both provide bridges to renewed understanding between the British and American peoples, bridges thrown up at a time when a great diplomatic rapprochement between the two nations was in the course of being cemented. The *fin de siècle* was notable, among other events, for the appearance of that gauche and impulsive figure, the posturing Kaiser Wilhelm II, whose bellicosity did more to improve long-strained British-American relations than the combined efforts of a long line of American secretaries of state and their counterparts at Whitehall. A Continental behemoth suddenly loomed on the world horizon, posing a formidable challenge to Britain's naval and maritime supremacy and threatening to upset the European power balance so delicately reassembled by the old Congress of Vienna and kept pasted together by subsequent compromise settlements. In the light of the mounting concern over Germany, the British found it expedient to overlook that variety of affronts they long suffered at the hands of America, affronts stemming from the latter's proprietary attitude toward the whole Western Hemisphere and her politically inspired concern over the cause of Ireland.

That historic and lasting entente with England, then inaugurated, found reflection on this side of the Atlantic in more dispassionate writing by historians about the Revolution. The old British Empire was now treated with greater objectivity, even with unabashed sympathy, the causes of the American Revolution were restudied in a less partisan atmosphere than earlier times, and the role of the long-maligned Tories was reappraised. The historical works of such writers as Moses Coit Tyler, Sydney George Fisher, and Claude Halstead Van Tyne reflected this renunciation of the older chauvinism and parochialism, along with a more balanced treatment of an ancient quarrel.

Most consequential in this reappraisal of the origins of the American Revolution have been the writings of the school of imperial historians, notably George Louis Beer and Charles M. Andrews, and, although he was primarily an institutional historian, the extensive investigations of Herbert L. Osgood and his students. While Sydney George Fisher sought to neutralize the moral and political conflict with a strongly pro-British point of view thinly concealed under a mask of dispassionate objectivity, the imperial scholars reached like conclusions but with more systematic documentation. Theirs was not entirely an original conception. Eighteenth-century historians like John Oldmixon, William Douglass, and even Thomas Hutchinson saw the empire whole. But the new school of imperial historians was both felicitous in its timing and notable for its breadth of scholarship. Standing at White-hall rather than in Boston or Philadelphia, these scholars embraced in their investigation some twenty-seven or so colonies whom they reported as enjoying various stages of self-government, quite unlike the traditionalists who had confined their attention to the thirteen littoral provinces that finally revolted.

The point of view that the history of America before 1783 was "colonial" rather than "American," as Charles M. Andrews considered it, led to enormous involvement in the mechanics of imperial administration. This school gave us illuminating digressions about the customs service and the treasury, the war and admiralty departments, and in that sense it has been peculiarly parochial and myopic.

It tends to lose leaders and principles in the thickets of bureaucratic orders, and by concentrating on administrative problems relieves everyone of culpability for the ultimate disaster.

Latter-day investigators have challenged some of the findings of the imperial school. With massive statistics Lawrence A. Harper would refute the conclusions of George L. Beer that the workings of the Navigation Acts were beneficent to the colonies, while O. M. Dickerson has revealed how faulty and corrupt administration, as much as misguided policy, aroused animosities in America. More recently, Lawrence H. Gipson, in his triumphant multivolumed study, *The British Empire before the American Revolution,* argues the need of the British government to streamline colonial administration after the last intercolonial war—"The Great War for Empire," as he calls it—and assembles massive statistics to prove that the colonists were not paying their share of the costs of empire and were undertaxed as compared with George III's subjects in Great Britain.[20] It is perfectly understandable that the English landed gentry should have been determined to shift the fiscal burden of empire so far as possible from their own pocketbooks to the colonials, but neither Gipson nor any other imperial historian has been able to demonstrate that the taxes finally adopted were well conceived or that the British administrators exhibited a statesmanlike grasp of the delicate and complex problem.

In sum, the scholars of the imperial school have compiled an essential compendium of information on how the British Empire was administered but they have not come up with the answers as to what caused the sudden breakdown in communication between the British and the American people.

Another approach to the American Revolution, nurtured in the Whig-Liberal party tradition and capitalizing on the more favorable climate for Anglo-American studies, was offered in the confident expectation that it had the answers to Britain's mishandling of her first empire. The Whig treatment in its full-blown form is exposed in the entertaining and often stirring pages of George Otto Trevelyan's multivolume work, *The American Revolution*.[21] Nephew and intimate of the great Macaulay and a distinguished Liberal party figure in his own right, Trevelyan had an unconcealed bias against Toryism. To Trevelyan there was right and wrong, black and white, and, as his son George Macaulay Trevelyan observed, "he did not take much account of nuances." In his pages the Patriots emerge perhaps too pure and undefiled even for current American tastes, and the North Ministry is painted with colors a bit too deep-dyed as a collection of rogues, scoundrels, and dunderheads. Whigs on both sides of the great ocean are portrayed as engaged in fighting for a concept of the British Constitution which the King and his supporters, with some justice, considered archaic; the sense of drama is heightened by these contrasts, while it is left for others to set the balance true. Trevelyan's diverting pages captured a frivolous and venal society, a corrupt political system, and a stubborn and myopic King—all set off against an idyllic, if not overidealized, picture of American society. It was truly a work in the great Whig tradition, one that Macaulay himself would have applauded unreservedly.

During the last generation Trevelyan and Lecky's views of the English government in the eighteenth century have been the subject of major revisionist judgments, largely as a result of the massive assault on the Whig interpretation launched by Sir Lewis Namier and pressed by his disciples. Since Trevelyan's day scholars have subjected the constitutional structure of England in the reign of George III to obsessively microscopic examination. Their conclusions have relevance to what was the nub of Trevelyan's argument—namely, that the system of corruption developed to a high degree under George III had resulted in subverting the original Constitution. While conceding that George III may have been more active as an election manager than his grandfather, Namier insists that the difference was one of degree only. He argues that at the beginning of the reign of George III the right of the King to choose whatever ministers he wished stood uncontested, and that while there was a Whig and a Tory mentality in 1760—one non-Namier historian speaks of a "new toryism"[22]—the party system did not exist, merely political factions. Against the conservative forces that threw in their lot with the government were now arrayed an evolving Parliamentary opposition contesting many traditional assumptions and looking toward a more liberal future.[23] That opposition was, however, badly split over the issue of Parliamentary supremacy, with Rockingham stubbornly standing by the principles of the Declaratory Act passed during his first ministry. Beyond reminding us that the two-party system, as we know it, and the principle of Cabinet responsibility postdate the American Revolution the Namierites decline to go.

The followers of Sir Lewis Namier would not deny the existence of influence, even of corruption. Through its system of patronage the Crown controlled the disposal of numerous posts, and admittedly one had to reckon with its influence. In fact, unless you were a member sitting for a private or pocket borough you could not be wholly free of it. Instead of stigmatizing corruption as undermining the Constitution, which was how Burke as well as Trevelyan viewed it, Sir Lewis Namier, who revered the British monarchy and adored the British Constitution, would accept these traditional corrupt practices as "a mark of English freedom and independence, for no one bribes where he can bully." Highly skeptical of altruism in politics, he expected to find neither honesty nor conviction, and he was not disappointed in his quest.

On this conflict the revisionists pass no moral judgment, unlike their Whig-minded predecessors of Victorian and Edwardian days, unless their complete lack of sympathy for the American side of the dispute reveals an innate bias at the start. They have been content with minute studies into the origins and background of members of Parliament—notably an encyclopedic account of each member serving in Parliament during the Revolutionary period[24] —and the disposal of patronage. Their critics caution that in following the close and tortuous course which the Namierites pursue one may well lose sight of the great political principles around which the various Whig factions rallied, and thereby fail to recognize that what contemporaries thought the British Constitution was has perhaps more relevance for the years of the American Revolution than what the principal actors should have thought about it had they known what we know today.

To an understanding of the American Revolution much of the genealogical diggings of the Namierites seems irrelevant and even immaterial. Their furiously atomistic efforts have stirred up interminable controversy over such insoluble and intrinsically trivial issues as the exact relationship between George III, the Duke of Newcastle, and the Earl of Bute in the early 1760's. The Namierites have put everyone under their microscope and, despite magnification, their subjects emerge as puny midgets quite incapable by themselves of shaking the foundations of empire. The Parliament they depict is dominated by rival factions and local interests and is preoccupied largely with domestic and parochial issues. In fact, the critical election of 1774 was fought mainly over local issues.[25] A composite portrait of little men scurrying around to subserve themselves, their families, and their retainers does nothing to support the argument of the imperial school of historians that the British government was both beneficent and far-sighted. The thicket of objective scholarship provides inadequate cover for their thinly disguised distaste for the American Revolution. That epoch the Namierites would put down not to tyranny but to a combination of weakness, vacillation, and irresolution—traits shared by Parliament and the Executive. Always there is the implication that a little decisiveness and a little more force at the right time would have dissolved the succession of crises and preserved the empire.

And what happens to George III, that "Royal Brute of Briton," whom Whig historians denounced as tyrannical and corrupt, and for whom the Declaration of Independence reserves its most eloquent and ringing indictment? A Namierite, the late Eric Robson, concludes that "a careful reading of the manuscript sources of the reign of King George III similarly contradicts many of the absurd conclusions that have been drawn about that much maligned monarch's attitude toward the American colonies, and on the dispute between them and Great Britain."[26] Yet the publication of the correspondence of George III reveals a monarch who, had he lived today, would be the perfect sitting duck for the amateur psychoanalyst. A manic-depressive, rigid, moralistic, and censorious, he appeared to casual acquaintances to be equable and reserved, whereas his intimates knew him to be hot-tempered, tense, and loquacious, to bear grudges, and to make a virtue of obstinacy. His close attention to his duties was admirable, if obsessive, but his minute, almost hourly, instructions to his ministers made him often appear as a downright meddler. A repressed husband and a tyrannical parent, George III was always teetering on the brink of a mental breakdown. Recently a pair of British physicians, without benefit of blood or urine analysis, have exonerated George III from the stain of insanity. Instead, they claim, he had a rare disease called porphyrinuria, which heretofore could only be established by demonstrating the presence of porphyrin in the urine of the patient. Granted this free-swinging diagnosis is accurate, it would now appear that George III was not really crazy. He only acted mad. When he broke down in 1788, used foul and indecent language, had to be kept away by force from the ladies of the court, and was confined to a strait jacket, it was all a symptom of this wonderfully strange disease.

George III's instability is not really the issue. Anyone who has studied the papers of the monarch and of the public men of this era knows that the King always had the last word, and that all major actions, military or diplomatic, awaited his personal decisions. And he was not reluctant to make them. His first minister, Lord North, however affable in manner and adroit in political management, was too evasive and irresolute to assume the mantle of war leader. While the direction of the war was a fragmented responsibility, such leadership as there was on the British side was assumed by the King. Speaking of the New England governments in late 1774, it was George III who held them to be "in a state of rebellion," and charged North that "blows must decide whether they are to be subject to this country or independent."[27] It was the King who, during the riotous days of June, 1780, issued a military proclamation and ordered the troops to fire on the mob, at a time when Lord North seemed to suffer from a paralysis of nerve. Again, and throughout the diplomatic negotiations for ending the war, it was George III who refused to allow outside mediators to intervene in what he considered a private quarrel between himself and his ungrateful children, the American insurgents. It was the King who drew back at every proposal to recognize the Thirteen States or to grant them independence, who personally spurned French peace feelers in the summer of 1780, which would have ended the war on terms far more favorable than anything England could later obtain. It was the King who could only be prevailed upon, by the clever maneuvering of Lord Shelburne, to digest the undigestible. Shelburne, who had succeeded Rockingham, by zigging and zagging finally persuaded a most reluctant monarch to bow to the inevitable and accept the cruel necessity of unconditional independence. When the King made the announcement before a packed Parliament he was visibly shaken and embarrassed, and almost choked on the words "free and independent states." Yes, well-meaning and basically moderate though he was, George III himself kept the initiative from the beginning to the end of the Revolution and it is not easy to exculpate him from blame.

And how about Lord George Germain? Many tears are wasted on him in Piers Mackesy's recent authoritative account of the war from the British point of view. But it does not really matter whether he was a coward, or a homosexual, or an incompetent. Indeed, he may have been innocent of all these monotonously repeated charges. What does matter are his opinions and the way he acted upon them. Did Germain mean it, or did he not, when he advised Parliament to put an end to the town meetings in Massachusetts, and thus snuff out grass-roots democracy? "You have, Sir, no government, no governor; the whole are the proceedings of a tumultuous and riotous rabble, who ought, if they had the least prudence, to follow their mercantile employment and not trouble themselves with politics and government, which they do not understand."[28] This was not the way Edmund Burke spoke in the same debates, when he argued "that a fair trial may be had in America" and that "a great black book and a great many red coats will never be able to govern it." Or Charles James Fox, who argued that it was more expedient to govern by management than by military force.[29] Here was a case where the issue was clearly joined over principle, and it really does not make the slightest difference whether Fox had had a successful evening at the gaming table at Brooks's the night before, or whether Burke had judgment debts against him in King's Bench for over £6,000.[30]

What have the Namierites left us of the principles so clearly articulated during the great debates over the coming and the conduct of the American Revolution? When Charles Van, in the debates in Parliament over the Coercive Acts, ventured the opinion that "Boston ought to be knocked about their ears and destroyed, *Delenda est Carthago!*" or, a few weeks later, when he advocated setting on fire the forests of Massachusetts to facilitate the punitive operation, did he mean it, or did he say it because, as Namier and Brooke point out in their encyclopedic account of Parliament, he had married into the influential Morgan family of Tredegar?[31]

Both in the waging of the war and in the making of the peace principles figured as prominently as men. The American Commissioners, acting upon instructions from Congress as well as upon their own principles, sought to incorporate into the Definitive Peace Treaty complete reciprocity between England and America, and with Shelburne they had a sympathetic listener. Did he not repeatedly insist that "we prefer trade to dominion," and that a peace was good "in the exact proportion that it recognizes" the principle of free trade?[32] Alas for reciprocal trade, Shelburne was out of office before he could implement his proposals, and William Eden, marshaling impressive protectionist arguments advanced by Lord Sheffield, attacked the reciprocal trade proposal as introducing "a total revolution in our commercial system." Eden was right. This new principle would in fact have worked a revolution in trade relations, and it was not until 1846, by which time the British manufacturing interests were sufficiently powerful, that Parliament was prepared for the revolution. Here the issue was not of men but of measures, not over a principle abstractly considered, but rather one that the powerful shipping interests supported in their own interest and at the expense of long-term favorable relations between the former colonies and the mother country.[33]

Neither the inquiry into the administrative structure of the empire and the armed forces nor the atomistic pursuit of the structure of politics holds the key to the American Revolution, which was fought over clearly articulated issues. Without denying other important facets of the Revolutionary movement, most present-day historians are prepared to accept the American Revolution for what it said it was—a political and constitutional struggle over sovereignty, a battle where who was right was more important than whose pocketbook was being pinched.

The concept of the American Revolution as centering about an ideological struggle is hardly novel. Thomas Jefferson, Tom Paine, and John Adams all looked upon the Revolution as the result of "a mental examination," a change "in the minds and hearts of the people."[34] Moses Coit Tyler, that pioneer historian of Revolutionary thought, described the American Revolution as "preeminently a revolution caused by ideas, and pivoted on ideas." Unlike the French Revolution, he pointed out, it was directed "not against tyranny inflicted, but only against tyranny anticipated."

After Tyler, a long line of historians in the Populist-Progressive tradition sought to puncture what they considered the myth that principle governed the Patriot party, to demonstrate that rhetoric was a cover for self-interest, and that reasoned arguments shifted ground, with the shifting countermoves of Parliament and Crown. Drawing heavily on Marxist thought and behaviorist psychology, the Populist-Progressive historians have been guilty of the fallacy of oversimplification. What appeared when freshly offered to be a rational explanation of a complex phenomenon now seems only a partial and heavily slanted analysis of the motives which prompt men to act in crisis situations.

At best the Populist-Progressive historians have given us insights into the zigzag course pursued by various interest groups without contributing much to clarifying the total picture. Even in this one area they have been challenged. Edmund S. Morgan in his analysis of the Stamp Act and in subsequent writings has argued that the colonists were consistent in their opposition to the Stamp Act, and with consistency contested, from the year 1765 down to the adoption of the Declaration of Independence, the authority of Parliament to tax them whether externally or internally. Perhaps the issue over internal versus external taxation was a synthetic rather than a real issue, but certain well-informed contemporaries like the scholarly Maryland lawyer Daniel Dulany, the worldly-wise Franklin, and Royalist Thomas Hutchinson put great score by the difference. With considerable cunning Charles Townshend thought that the distinction offered a way out. Grafton tells us of Townshend's boast in Parliament that he knew the mode by which a revenue might be drawn from America *without offense*.[35] Of course, he was self-deceived in believing that the colonists who opposed the Stamp Act would accept external levies for revenue purposes. What the colonists were objecting to was taxation without representation, whether direct or indirect. By this date, as John Dickinson's *Farmer's Letters* make clear, the colonists saw the real issue as centering on the authority of Parliament to tax for revenue as contrasted with its right to impose duties for the regulation of commerce. The constitutional power to impose the latter was clearly conceded in America down to the year 1774, by which time a galaxy of American intellectuals, including James Wilson, Thomas Jefferson, John Adams, and young

Alexander Hamilton, denied *in toto* Parliament's legislative authority.

What the Patriot intellectuals were attempting to do was to refashion the empire to give America a substantial measure of self-determination, but the successful implementing of their proposals depended upon the helm of state being firmly in the grasp of bold and creative statesmen, able both to reshape Parliamentary thinking and to persuade a stubborn monarch. Those conditions did not obtain. Instead of conciliating, Parliament, under prodding from the Ministry, tried coercion. By declaring New England to be in a state of rebellion and by escalating its punitive measures and soft-pedaling its conciliatory proposals, the British government left the colonies little alternative but to part company with the empire. Some of those who did forswear allegiance to George III were fifth- and sixth-generation descendants of original colonizers. The bonds may no longer have been close, but the tie was still hard to sunder.

To accept the notion of a republic and its innate superiority to monarchy required years of intellectual preparation. The ideological elements which entered into the transforming radicalism of the American Revolution have most recently been considered by Bernard Bailyn in his magisterial introduction to his welcome edition of *Pamphlets of the American Revolution*. Spelling out in closer detail the documentation of Ramsay and Tyler, Bailyn picks out the variety of intellectual threads which were woven into the pattern of arguments of opposing sides, beginning with the sermon of Jonathan Mayhew in 1750, his renowned "Discourse Concerning Unlimited Submission," which quickly won recognition as a classic formulation of the necessity and virtue of resistance to oppression. This new pamphlet collection attests to the importance of classical influences in shaping the Revolutionary mind, to the weight accorded Enlightenment writers, from Locke to Rousseau, to the characteristic resort to arguments drawn from England's legal history as the Revolutionary pamphleteers misconstrued it, and to the special values derived from the covenant theology of New England Puritanism. Taking his cue from Ramsay, Bailyn has demonstrated the heavy debt of some American pamphleteers to English radical thinkers of the early eighteenth century, particularly to men like John Trenchard and Thomas Gordon, coauthors of *Cato's Letters*. Arguments derived from classical thought and Calvinist theology, buttressed by frequent resort to common law, to the natural rights philosophy, and to the Whig party line, were all woven into the patterned texture of the Revolutionary ideology.

Apart from these sources of Revolutionary thought, Mr. Bailyn lays great stress upon "the fear of a comprehensive conspiracy against liberty throughout the English-speaking world." Now, we have become quite familiar with conspiracies. Richard Hofstadter has given us a penetrating analysis of the paranoid state of mind which has dominated the radical Right from McCarthy to the Birchites. But the roots of paranoia lie much deeper. They can be unearthed in America at the time of the French Revolution and demonstrated to have fueled the fires of nativist agitation in the nineteenth century. These later examples have a good deal more clinical significance, however, than those derived from the Revolutionary era. Much of the language of "conspiracy" can be put down to rhetoric. Serious men gave little credence to it. In both England and America the opposing sides recklessly charged their adversaries with conspiring to subvert the particular Constitution each wished to preserve. Granted that mutual suspicion infected the dialogue of the time, it is dubious whether sensible and sophisticated men put much stock in such talk, and even if they did, such paranoiac charges hurled from opposing sides would have canceled each other out. In the battle of ideas the corroding distrust of the parties stemmed from the divergent views of the British Constitution which they championed. The American Whigs, like their English counterparts, fought for the concept of the English Constitution that had emerged from the Revolution of 1688. The Royalists upheld the Constitution as it appeared to have evolved by 1760. That was the nub of that irreconcilable conflict of ideas from which there seemed no recourse but revolution. In this respect, and in the sense that it was rooted in observance of law, the American Revolution may be labeled a conservative political revolution.

If the partisans of revolution were conservatives, they could hardly be counted as consistent ones. How could one defy one's monarch and be ranked as a conservative? The Revolutionary partisans fought for the concept of a republican order founded upon the principle of government by consent, and that subtle concept holds as many seminal and revolutionary elements as does the concept of federalism which many of the same Revolutionary leaders utilized to forge a durable republican order extending over a vast domain of territory.

If they were agreed on one point, the Founding Fathers were united in regarding their Revolution as antimonarchical. So Jefferson envisaged the central issue, not only in drafting the Declaration of Independence but in retrospective comments on the party strife in post-Revolutionary years.[36] On more than one occasion John Jay, exposed to the trappings of monarchy in unfriendly Spain, was perhaps surprised to find how staunch a republican he had become. At Aranjuez, the flower-scented summer residence of the Spanish royal family, Jay was shocked at the military establishment which the monarch deemed necessary to assure his physical safety. "Soldiers, with fixed bayonets," Jay remarked, "present themselves at various stations in these peaceful retreats; and though none but inoffensive citizens are near, yet horsemen with drawn swords, guarding one or other of the royal family in their little excursions to take the air daily, renew and impress ideas of subjection." How unlike a day's fishing by a couple of New England selectmen. Again, in a recently deciphered portion of a letter to Congress, written in a mood reflecting his bitterness and frustration in the role of unaccredited American minister to Spain, Jay remarked: "I shall be disappointed if I find Courts moving on any other principle, than political ones, and indeed, not always on those. Caprice, whim, the interests and passions of individuals, must and will always have greater or less degree of influence." By this date his experience at the various Spanish courts had confirmed him in his staunch republicanism. "We shall always be deceived," Jay warned, "if we believe that any nation in the world has, or will have, a disinterested regard for us, especially absolute monarchies, where the temporary views or passions of the Prince, his Ministers, his women, or his favorites, not the voice of the people, direct the helm."[37]

Perhaps, if he were cross-examined, Jay would have qualified his comment by saying "the voice of the *informed* people," but for an élitist aristocrat who had been impelled to assume a revolutionary posture, to commit treason against his King, and to mouth the rhetoric of democracy, John Jay, the conservative New York lawyer, had by the year 1780 traveled a long road. So had the revolutionary leadership in general. The Revolution had taken place above all within their own minds. And there was no turning back.

NOTES TO CHAPTER I

1. See, e.g., Francisco A. Encina, *Historia de Chile desde la prehistoria hasta 1891* (20 vols., Santiago, 1941–1952), VI, 7–15; Sir Charles K. Webster, ed., *Britain and the Independence of Latin America, 1812–1830: Select Documents from the Foreign Office* (London, 1938), I, 6–12; also R. A. Humphreys and John Lynch, *The Origins of the Latin American Revolutions, 1808–1826* (New York, 1965); Charles Gibson, *Spain in America* (New York, 1966).

2. *On Revolution* (New York, 1963), p. 49.

3. R. R. Palmer, *The Age of the Democratic Revolution,* (2 vols., Princeton, N.J., 1959, 1964).

4. *Collected Works,* ed. by R. P. Basler (New Brunswick, N.J., 1933), VI, 434 (July 4, 1861).

5. George Santayana, *Persons and Places: The Middle Span* (Boston, 1945), p. 169.

6. See Isaiah Berlin, *Historical Inevitability* (London, 1954).

7. *The Adams-Jefferson Letters,* ed. Lester J. Cappon (2 vols., Chapel Hill, N.C., 1959), II, 455.

8. The most recent recognition of the rapid maturation of the colonies in this period is found in L. H. Gipson, *The British Empire before the American Revolution* (New York, 1961), X, 3–37. For historiographic summary, *ibid.,* XIII (1967).

9. *The African Trade the Great Pillar and Support of the British Plantation Trade in America* (London, 1745).

10. Thomas Gage, *Correspondence,* ed. by C. E. Carter (New Haven, 1931–1933), II, 450.

11. See William Nelson, *The American Tory* (Oxford, 1961), pp. 76–78, 180.

12. Gipson, *British Empire* (New York, 1965), XII, 39.

13. David Ramsay, *The History of the American Revolution* (Philadelphia, 1789), I, 112–113.

14. *Memoirs of George II, I,* 397.

15. Sir Lewis Namier and John Brooke, *Charles Townshend* (London, 1964), p. 37.

16. *Ibid.,* pp. 129, 130.

17. *Ibid.,* pp. 179 *et seq.*

18. John Higham, "The Cult of an American Consensus," *Amer. Hist. Rev.,* LXVIII (1962), 610 *et seq.;* J. Rogers Hollingsworth, "Consensus and Continuity in Recent American Historical Writing," *South Atlantic Quarterly,* LXI (1962), 40 *et seq.;* Jack P. Greene, "The Flight from Determinism," *Ibid.,* pp. 235 *et seq.*

19. David Ramsey, *History of the American Revolution* (Lexington, Ky., 1815), I, 40, 41.

20. See also the table on approximate tax burden per head in Palmer, *Age of the Democratic Revolution,* I, 155.

21. Recently the present writer has issued a one-volume condensation (New York, 1964; London, 1966).

22. G. H. Guttridge, *English Whiggism and the American Revolution* (Berkeley and Los Angeles, 1963), p. 15.

23. See J. R. Christie, "Was there a 'New Toryism' in the Earlier Part of George III's Reign?" *Journal of British Studies,* V (1965), 60–76.

24. Sir Lewis Namier and John Brooke, *The History of Parliament: The House of Commons, 1754–1790* (3 vols., New York, 1964).

25. See Bernard Donoughue, *British Politics and the American Revolution: the Path to War, 1773–1775* (New York, 1964).

26. Eric Robson, *The American Revolution, 1763–1783* (London, 1955), p. 17.

27. W. B. Donne, ed., *Correspondence of George III with Lord North* (London, 1867), I, 214.

28. Cobbett, *Parl. Hist.*, XVII, 1195–1196.

29. *Ibid.*, 1313–1315.

30. Namier and Brooke, *op. cit.*, II, 156.

31. Cobbett, *op. cit.*, XVII, 1178; Namier and Brooke, *op. cit.*, III, 572.

32. Shelburne to Abbé Morellet, March 13, 23; Morellet to Shelburne, April 1, 1783. Lansdowne Papers, Bowood; Morellet, *Mémoires*, I, 288.

33. R. B. Morris, *The Peacemakers* (New York, 1965), pp. 429 *et seq.*

34. Thomas Paine, Letter to Abbé Raynal (1782) in Philip S. Foner, ed., *Complete Writings of Thomas Paine* (New York, 1945), II, 243; John Adams to H. Niles, Feb. 13, 1818, in *Works,* ed. by C. F. Adams (Boston, 1850–1856), X, 282.

35. Sir William R. Anson, ed., *Autobiography and Political Correspondence of Augustus Henry, third duke of Grafton* (London, 1898), pp. 126–127.

36. Jefferson, *Writings,* ed. by P. L. Ford (New York, 1904), I, 166–167.

37. John Jay to Robert Morris, April 25, 1782, Windsor Castle Archives; to President of Congress, Nov. 6, 1780. John Jay Letterbook, Huntington Library.

II

THE TWO
REVOLUTIONS

It has been fashionable of late to regard the American
Revolution as a war for political independence, and nothing more than that, to minimize the social changes that it
effected or that followed in its wake. To accept the American Revolution for what it *primarily* was, a political war
for independence rather than a *sans-culotte* type of uprising, does not entitle us to consign so momentous a
struggle to the category of status revolts, to consider it as
indistinguishable from that long series of conflicts in Latin
America of *creoles* against *peninsulares* which resulted in
a shift of political power without effecting basic social
adjustments. Obviously, all the eighteenth-century revolutions of the Western world provided lessons for later
revolutionary movements,[1] and not least of all, the American. The first of the great revolutions provided the impulse and served as the example for all that followed, but
the later ones have marked points of difference.

With considerable persistence recent analysts have
viewed the American Revolution as a museum piece.

They have come upon an isolated rivulet which, so they say, never does force its way down to join the broad stream of revolutionary movements that have transformed the modern world. One recent student of revolutions looks upon the American Revolution as having been seemingly "achieved in a kind of ivory tower into which the fearful spectacle of human misery, the haunting voice of abject poverty, never penetrated."[2] Another sees it as nothing more than "the orderly transference of allegiance from one set of magistrates to a slightly different set who happened to be called representatives of the people."[3] In the latter sense political scientists of the standing of Louis Hartz, Clinton Rossiter, and Daniel Boorstin would deny that there was any American Revolution. Since Americans did not have to fight for freedom, but were born free, and did not have to be liberated from a feudal status, having escaped feudalism by coming to America, their war for independence, according to these writers' argument, is invested with overtones of traditionalism and constitutionalism that set it apart from the class struggles that have divided the Old World.[4]

One need not grant all these premises to concede that the American Revolution has two overriding elements not found in the French Revolution or in those which were shaped in its design. They are *consensus* and *continuity*. The American Revolution found quick acceptance once it was over, and the constitutional structure that was its end product has, save for one terribly divisive war, withstood the test of time as has no other constitution forged in the modern world.

We accept it, and do not need to be reminded of it. Save for Independence Hall and Bunker Hill Monument there are few visible memorials of this transforming event. In Washington's Lafayette Park the Marquis and the Comte de Rochambeau stand today in postures of watchful waiting, apparently expecting a call to the White

House at any moment. And then, of course, there is Washington Monument, the Jefferson Memorial, and Mount Vernon not far away. But that is all at our national capital. In New York one has to be a detective first grade to locate the plaques commemorating the battles of Golden Hill and Harlem Heights.

Unlike New York, which has no single avenue named after a person or event of the Revolution, Paris constantly reminds its people of their great revolution. There is a Place de la Bastille, a Place de la Concorde, and a Place de la République. There are streets commemorating the Twenty-ninth of July and the Fourth of September and revolutionary leaders like Danton, Robespierre, and even the implacable Saint-Just. We have no Fourth of July Plaza, only Union Square.

Paradoxical as it may seem, although Parisians are constantly reminded of their Revolution, they are by no means reconciled to it. In France, unlike the United States, the Revolution which created the modern nation is still a live and continuing issue in national politics. Everybody who remained in America accepted the American Revolution from the time independence was grudgingly acknowledged by George III, and if there have been divisions in American politics over states' rights, sectionalism, the tariff, slavery, and the welfare state, these divisive issues were unrelated to that paramount event in our history, the Revolution which gave the United States independence and national identity.

Were one of those ubiquitous pollsters to ask a random sampling of Americans today, "Do you think the American Revolution was worthwhile?" the answer invariably would be: "Of course, that's obvious." Differ though the Daughters of the American Revolution may with Walter Reuther or Martin Luther King as to what our Revolution stands for, nobody doubts its virtue.

In France, on the other hand, the extreme Right has

always insisted that the French Revolution was a tragic mistake, or went too far; the extreme Left, that it did not go far enough. As a result of this polarization of extremes over an historical issue, the Revolution has been constantly subverted by the Right and is still being championed by the Left. Profound social and economic explanations have been advanced to explain why the French Revolution veered off course and has been a tragic failure, while the American remained true to its central objectives and has been vindicated by the course of history. A preoccupation with consequences has led us to ignore the starting points of the two revolutionary movements and to overlook the fact that in their origins they had much in common. The Declaration of Independence and the constitution making by the states inspired the Tennis Court Oath which the Third Estate took, vowing that it would not disband before a constitution was drafted and accepted by the monarch. But the Revolution in France soon dissolved into an avalanche of constitutions, until the whole notion of constitutionalism was discredited beyond recognition.

Both Revolutions in origin arose out of disputes over taxation. In America the initial dispute over Parliament's right to tax escalated into a repudiation of the monarchy and an assertion of independence from the British Empire. In France a movement of internal reform to deal with ominously rising national deficits (attributed in no small part to France's handsome aid to the American patriots in their revolution) soon mounted a foreign war, overthrew the monarchy, nationalized the church and took over its property, broadened land distribution to the peasants, reformed the laws, and extended the suffrage.

These ends were achieved, however, only at the price of anarchy, civil war, terror, and the heritage of a divided nation. Granted that conditions in the two nations at the time of their respective revolutions were very different, the contrast in the results of the movements may be imputed in no small part to the contrast in leadership. In America the unstable and fiery James Otis and the astute if demagogic Samuel Adams may have lighted the fires of revolution, but a much more solid and responsible leadership seized the helm.

In France the story was quite the reverse. The aristocrats, who may be said to have begun it, men like Lafayette and Mirabeau, were torn between loyalty to the King and a sincere desire for reform, and ended by being distrusted by both the Left and the Right. The men who supplanted them were far more doctrinaire and extreme and had extravagant defects of character for which the French nation has paid a fearful toll. The dynamic and eloquent Danton constantly sold himself to the highest bidder. The enemy who supplanted him, the chaste and sober Robespierre, was corrupted by his own enormous vanity; the man who believed that "Virtue is powerless without Fear" could shed blood without scruple.

That the French Revolution was transformed into a military dictatorship was due in large measure to the fact that there was no leader in France of the stature of George Washington, no one who was prepared to renounce power when the major goals had been achieved, no one who dared speak out as Washington did to the army officers in March, 1783, demanding that they express "horror and detestation" at the possibility of a military coup against the civil authorities.

If the American Revolution has been considered as the classic example of a political revolution stressing principles of orderly change and constitutionalism, the French Revolution, contrariwise, stands as the classic model for social revolutions which arrayed class against class. Both these images happen to be facile oversimplifications, but they have never been erased from either the public memory or the judgment of serious scholars. Thus, it is argued that the French Revolution raised the social question and transformed a struggle for the Rights of Man into one for the rights of the Sans-Culottes,[5] whereas no such turning point marked the course of the American Revolution. The French Revolution, argues Hannah Arendt, was deflected from its legal course by "the immediacy of suffering," and it was determined "by the exigencies of liberation not from tyranny but from necessity." Whether that necessity which injected a shrill and hysterical note into the French Revolution was mass poverty or the threat of foreign military intervention, Miss Arendt does not pause to consider. One need not decide the hotly contested issue whether France was prosperous or in the throes of an economic crisis at the end of the *ancien régime.* Regardless of the extent of agrarian misery, regardless of how rapidly prices may have outraced wages, the nation's revolutionary crisis stemmed initially from fiscal difficulties rather than mass hunger.[6] The situation is not unfamiliar to us today. In New York and other great urban centers we have an affluent society dwelling in and around cities which are periodically confronted by fiscal bankruptcy. Surely it is not proposed to bring back the ghost of M. Necker to solve America's urban problems, but it is submitted that the analogy is not as farfetched as it may seem at first glance.

It is not poverty but rising expectations that impel people to revolt. Revolutions seldom if ever recruit their leaders from the lower classes but normally propel to the fore people with middle-class aspirations who for one reason or another find the door to opportunity or security closed. Such was the case in both the American and the French Revolutions.

Both revolutions were started by élites, but the fact that in America the same élite that began the Revolution remained in control at the end has given to the American a deceptively conservative coloration which the French

Revolution has never pretended to assume. From James Otis to Henry Laurens, the Patriot leadership consisted of men of standing and influence, hardly the dispossessed, and constituted perhaps the most conservative leadership that any revolution ever confessed. We shall, then, have to agree with Alexander Graydon's judgment that "the opposition to the claim of Britain originated with the better sort: it was truly aristocratical in its commencement." But this was not a point of difference with the French Revolution, although the two pursued divergent courses. Referring to the latter, Chateaubriand wrote: "The patricians began the Revolution. The plebeians finished it."

Certainly in their beginnings the two revolutions had strong points of similarity. Both stressed legality. Both affirmed the rights of man and the sacredness of private property. In fact in some respects the French Revolution at its inception was more conservative and legalistic than the American, for the National Assembly provided compensation for the abolition of substantial feudal dues, whereas, save for the Penn estates and the proprietary lands of Henry Harford in Maryland, no state legislature made provision for compensating any Tory whose estates were confiscated. As in the American Revolution, aside from church lands, the only estates confiscated were those of the émigrés. Large landowners who did not commit acts against the Revolution were untouched. Furthermore, in both revolutions there was a strong peasant support for the conservative side. As many as 70 percent of those condemned in the Terror were members of the peasant and laboring classes prosecuted for activities against the state, and in the American Revolution the back-country farmer in areas like New York and the Carolinas was strongly Tory.

Despite their parallel legalistic beginnings, the two revolutions took divergent paths. The American Revolution took a Whig-Girondin course rather than a Jacobin.

There was no Terror. There was no Thermidor. Perhaps this was in part because fiscal and social grievances were not as acute in America as in France, and that class hatreds were not rooted in centuries of exploitation as under the *ancien régime*. Perhaps, too, we are more conscious today of the totalitarian implications of the French Revolutionary Left than were our fathers who did not know totalitarianism,[7] but even so leftist a Revolutionary as Tom Paine remained at heart a petit bourgeois and was as unsympathetic to the Communist world of Babeuf as a Washington, a Hamilton, or an Edmund Burke. In justice to the French Revolution it should be added that the extremism of its later stages was not entirely and inevitably the consequence of the movement but in considerable measure a response to foreign intervention, to a counter-revolutionary element that was not present to the same degree in the American Revolution.

In their inception both the American and French Revolutions sought to re-establish some idealized version of a constitutional order believed once to have existed. The British Constitution which the American Patriots thought they were fighting to uphold was in fact an instrument of oligarchical power. The constitutional liberties which the Americans asserted and reasserted had virtually all been won by 1689, while the British Constitution which the North Ministry and the Parliamentary majority upheld was the instrument of government that had evolved under the Hanoverians, with its reassertion of monarchical power and prestige. Similarly, as Georges Lefebvre has shown,[8] the first act of the French Revolution in 1788 dramatized an attempt by the aristocracy to win back the political authority of which the Bourbon dynasty had despoiled it. The difference between the two revolutions lay in the fact that, once having defied royal authority, the Whig leadership which started the war in America kept control of the machinery of war and then made the peace;

whereas in France the aristocracy, having paralyzed the royal power which had upheld its own social pre-eminence, lost its grip on the movement, and there ensued, in turn, according to the now popular simplistic interpretation of Lefebvre, a bourgeois revolution, a popular revolution in the cities, and finally a revolt of the peasants. This alleged sequence of class developments never manifested itself in the American Revolution.

Hence, the notion rapidly spread that the American Revolution was conservative in aim and development and somehow different from the French. Historians from the time of Friedrich Gentz to that of Daniel Boorstin and political thinkers from Edmund Burke down to Russell Kirk have stressed the idea of the American Revolution as a conservative force, with perhaps more of Maistre and less of Voltaire than has been popularly understood. Gentz regarded the American Revolution as a *defensive* revolution in contrast to the French Revolution, which he saw as *offensive*. To the Prussian the former had a fixed object and operated within definite limits and inside the confines of legality. As he saw it, the American Revolution was "not made, but prevented." Many writers from Burke down to the present have taken the same position, but it is perhaps significant that the Tory Jonathan Boucher, admittedly a biased observer, disputed this conception and denied that "in point of principle there is a shade of difference between the American Revolution and the French rebellion."[9] From the point of view of a Loyalist or an émigré who had lost everything Boucher's sweeping generalization made a good deal of sense.

The more extreme wing of the French Revolutionary movement would have agreed with Gentz and disputed Boucher. As Babeuf saw it, society was torn by an incessant, although mostly silent, civil war, but when the people's rights to the fulfillment of the conditions of the Social Contract have been denied by a few engrossers, then a struggle between the "haves" and "have-nots" becomes inevitable. To the Babeuvists the French not the American Revolution marked the beginning of an apocalyptic hour in mankind's history when at long last man would achieve real equality. To them the French Revolution was a total revolution. Contrariwise, those ideologues Marx and Engels regarded the American Revolution not as a struggle of poor against rich but rather as a bourgeois movement of liberation, and Marxist historians, from Jean Jaurès to Albert Mathiez, have similarly accented the bourgeois character of the French Revolution.

Indubitably much data can be adduced to support the interpretation of both the American and French Revolutions as bourgeois movements of liberation, and some recent respectable opinion so holds.[10] The leadership of the Sons of Liberty, the membership of the Committees of Correspondence, of the Revolutionary state legislatures, and of the Second Continental Congress were heavily recruited from businessmen, lawyers, and the landowning gentry who were in fact entrepreneurial operators to whom land offered a chance for speculative gains rather than a way of preserving or enhancing social status.

French Revolutionary leadership had many points of similarity to American. As Crane Brinton's investigation has disclosed, above 60 percent of the membership of the Jacobin clubs, in both the moderate and the violent phases of the French Revolution, were recruited from the middle class, and a sizable number of the bourgeoisie managed to keep in good standing in both the Girondin and Montagnard phases of the Revolution.[11]

The thesis that the American Revolution was fought to liberate the middle class is certainly debatable; on the other hand, there is no denying that the lifting of the restraints of the Navigation Laws had a dramatic impact on the patterns of trade and industry.[12] The war itself made rich men richer and enhanced the economic position of privateers, army contractors, and those who managed to combine public interest with private profit. When Barbé-Marbois informed Vergennes that in America "the prospect of peace has given more general discontent than anything that has happened in a long time; particularly among the mercantile part of the community," he combined a spice of malice with a shrewd observation on the stake of the *nouveaux riches* in the continuance of the war.[13]

Both revolutions, in seeking to protect and sanctify property rather than to abolish it, confessed their basically middle-class objectives. The Massachusetts Provincial Congress called upon the Continental Congress to recommend setting up civil governments in the states, urging that "there are in many parts of the colony alarming symptoms of the abatement of the sense in the minds of some people of the sacredness of private property, which is plainly assignable to the want of civil government; and your honors must be fully sensible that a community of goods and estates will soon be followed by the utter waste and destruction of the goods themselves."[14] Although this commentary takes on some of the shrill overtones of General Knox's later leveling charges against the Shaysites,[15] it is clear that the American Revolution may have had its Levelers, as the English Revolution before it, but there is no evidence to substantiate the view that it had its agrarian communists or "Diggers."[16] A widespread respect for the rights of property was reflected in such basic Revolutionary charters as the Virginia Bill of Rights, with its assertion of the "means of acquiring and possessing property" as an inherent right, and in the Massachusetts Constitution of 1780, affirming the right of each individual to be protected in the enjoyment of his life, liberty, and property, "according to the standing laws."

Those who have examined the ideologies and probed the hidden motives of American Patriot leaders, even of

admittedly atypical figures like Ethan Allen, have shown
how John Locke was Americanized to give support to the
notion that governments were organized to protect property, that corrupt governments attempting to undermine
property might rightly be overthrown, and new governments set up in their place guaranteeing the sanctity of
property. All this was presented in less naked form so that
the myth of the yeoman farmer might be perpetuated and
the interests of incipient capitalists and land speculators
shown to be jeopardized by powerful interests controlling
government.[17] To a goodly number, but by no means all,
the American Revolution was a movement to fulfill aspirations to acquire more property.

The rapidity with which the fruits of revolution were
accepted once the war was won has prompted that perceptive historian of the Enlightenment, J. Salwyn Scha-
piro, to contrast the American War for Independence
with the French, the former being "digested," the latter
"undigested," and has inspired Clinton Rossiter to talk of
an "American consensus." To what extent that "American
consensus" rests on the fact that a very numerous dissenting element, the Loyalists, was eliminated, and that these
émigrés, unlike those of France, were never, with minor
exceptions, permitted to return, is an interesting subject of
speculation.[18]

Striking though the similarities are between the American and the French Revolutions, the two movements have
obvious differences, as obvious as the contrast in the
characters and temperaments of a Washington and a
Robespierre. The trouble is that recent commentators
have made the differences appear more obvious than the
facts warrant. They have refused to give to the American
Revolution any dimension other than that of a political
movement of liberation, whereas they have invested the
French Revolution with all the trappings of class war.

Now, in order to have a class war you have to have

fairly distinct classes and those below must have a deep sense of exploitation by those above. Recent historians simply refuse to press American colonial society into such a mold. They see nothing but homogeneity, equality, and bland contentment. To Louis Hartz, for example, the difference between the bourgeois revolution in America and those that followed consists in the fact that America skipped the feudal stage of history. Hartz concedes the survival of such "aspects of the decadent feudalism of the later period" as primogeniture, entails, and quitrents, but insists that since America does not have a feudal tradition it does not have a socialist tradition. "The *ancien régime*," he asserts, "inspires Rousseau; both inspire Marx."[19] Others have found in America an air of rusticity, simplicity, and equality that was not consonant with a highly structured class system, which arrayed conspicuous wealth and privilege against abject poverty and servility. Indeed, to these analysts, American Revolutionary society was marvelously "seamless."[20]

In evaluating the extent of equality and a class structure in the American colonies much depends on one's vantage point. The Revolutionary diplomats dispatched to Europe were shocked at the abysmal poverty they found abroad. Traveling across northern Spain in mid-January of 1780 through frost, snow, and ice, John Adams observed the poverty and economic sluggishness of the Spanish countryside. He saw men, women, and children "with naked legs and feet, standing on the cold stones in the mud, by the hour together." He journeyed through crumbling villages of mud and straw, and noted an impoverished countryside exploited by "Church, State and Nobility." When he crossed the border to Saint-Jean-de-Luz, Adams commented: "Never was captive escaped from prison more delighted than I was." If France by comparison with Spain was both affluent and comfortable, America to this lonely New Englander seemed like a Paradise

Lost. Two years before the French Revolution Jefferson, then American minister to the Court of Versailles, observed that "of twenty millions of people . . . there are nineteen millions more wretched, more accursed in every circumstance of human existence than the most conspicuously wretched individual of the whole United States."

Thus, America with its lack of a titled aristocracy, its widely distributed freehold, and its large English-speaking Protestant population had a deceptive homogeneity and classlessness. On the surface there was justification for Jefferson's boast that American citizens were "untainted by pride of rank."[21] If one probed just below the surface one would find islands, such as between the Lehigh and the Susquehanna, where only German, or a corrupted Germanic jargon, was spoken, or parts of the interior of the Carolinas where Highland Scots conversed only in Gaelic, or communities in the Hudson Valley where Dutch was still the language of the people and even of the courts.

If one probed still more deeply one would discover that the American colonists had fled the inequalities of Old World society only to create a society which differed more in degree than in form from the ancestral mold. Classes existed, but save for the Negro slave they were not so deeply etched on the landscape of the New World as on the Old, and the barriers proved far less restrictive. The great reservoir of untapped land offered a potential of vertical mobility, but nonetheless something of the deference for the wealthy, the influential, and the wellborn that pervaded European society was also present in America. From the beginning colonists paid attention to titles. The appellation "esquire" denominated a man of high economic rank, "gentleman," a person of somewhat lesser wealth, and "goodman," "goodwife," or "goody," normally a small yeoman farmer or his spouse. "Mr." was rather indiscriminately used, but generally designated a person of middling fortune.

True, American society was not rigid or ossified but was in a state of flux, with the degree of stratification varying from region to region. In New England, for example, where considerable equality in landholding prevailed and the yeoman subsistence farmer represented the typical settler, social rank counted, though for less than in New York or the Southern plantations. The proprietors of Wallingford, Connecticut, for example, gave to every "high rank man, or his hairs" 476 acres, to each "middel rank" 238 acres. In Kent, Connecticut, settled in 1738 by forty families, there was a considerable measure of equality, but in the course of time the workings of divisible succession led to impoverishment and inequality. Many third-generation inhabitants of that town, as the late Charles S. Grant has shown in a seminal study, inherited only one twentieth of their grandfathers' proprietary holdings and could definitely be classed as "poor."[22] Throughout New England the assignment of church pews reflected social rank, as did one's listing on the roster of Harvard College. Furthermore, while the property qualifications for voting did not in fact prove particularly restrictive—something that Thomas Hutchinson and George Bancroft had understood long before Robert Brown painstakingly re-established the fact—local communities showed great deference to the leadership and to the opinions of the principal personages and families, What one had in effect was a political democracy manipulated by an élite.

If a middle class of small property owners prevailed in subsistence farming areas, a more sharply differentiated class structure could be found in commercial farming country like the Hudson and Delaware Valleys, the Chesapeake estates, and the plantations of the Lower South. In upstate New York tenancy was of significant dimension, and one might say that the patroon families of that province, along with great landholders like the Livingstons, the Schuylers, and the De Lanceys, enjoyed an inordinate degree of political power in addition to high social pres-

tige. There was little to differentiate the political factionalism which divided New York between the party of the
De Lanceys and the party of the Livingstons from the
kind of factionalism organized in Parliament around such
landed aristocrats as the Duke of Bedford or the Mar-
quess of Rockingham or Lord Shelburne.

At the time of the Revolution the upper class in Virginia included the old established aristocracy of inherited
wealth and a small proportion of self-made men. Although
recent investigators would argue that Virginia was an
egalitarian democracy, dominance of the aristocracy was
implicitly accepted.[23] This society gave to the cause of
the American Revolution a remarkable group of planter-
politician-statesmen. Somewhat more recently formed
than Virginian, Carolina society numbered considerably
more *nouveaux riches,* and the fortunes of some leading
planters dwarfed most others in the American colonies.
Henry Middleton, for example, possessed an estate of
50,000 acres and 800 slaves, and around 1750 had an
annual income of at least £1,500 sterling, an enormous
fortune in those days. In contrast, the proportion of landless whites and squatters, mostly illiterate and politically
inarticulate, was greater in the frontier of the Carolinas
than elsewhere in the Thirteen Colonies.

Wherever tenancy or indentured servitude was the
prevailing method of farm labor, social distinctions would
be more intensified than in other regions. Tenancy was
more likely to be found in upstate New York, in Virginia's
Northern Neck, and in the western counties of Maryland,
in all of which areas land had been engrossed in parcels
and withheld from sale. In the Chesapeake area a very
small group of entrepreneurial planters, living ostenta-
tiously in the grand tradition, managed through shrewd
speculation to pick up huge grants of land in the back
country available for privileged insiders. The landlords of
the wild lands leased them to tenants who paid rents

while improving their leaseholds by clearing, planting orchards, and erecting houses, barns, and fences. As Aubrey Land has recently shown, over a third of the planters in the lowest £100 bracket in Maryland leased their land. This does not mean that the poor folk, even the indentured servants, were denied some share in the general prosperity of the Chesapeake. At least four persons in the latter category are known to have moved up from poverty, even from indentured servitude, to the top bracket of wealth, but for the mass advance was, by comparison with the affluent, glacial. There was indubitably a shift toward a higher standard of living for all whites dwelling in the Chesapeake area, but the two lowest categories of property owners still made up almost 91 percent of the planting families in the decades 1730–1739 as compared with a little over 96 percent forty years earlier.[24]

In colonial cities the class contrast was even more marked. There prosperous merchants dwelling in handsome Georgian homes provided a stark contrast to the mobile labor population comprising seamen, porters, carters, servants, apprentices, and even the unemployed, for by the middle of the eighteenth century this last group was beginning to pose a problem to town administrators. In the larger towns one found a considerable concentration of property. Jackson Turner Main has estimated that on the eve of the Revolution 10 percent of the largest real estate owners held 44 percent of the total value of all land in Albany, 5 percent in Boston, and in Philadelphia the top 10 percent paid two thirds of the taxes.[25] In colonial seaports the full force of nonimportation hit the seamen and harbor workers, long victimized by impressment for the Royal Navy, and these groups constituted a hard core of protest against British revenue measures.

It is a pity to mar the charming landscape of social affability and homogeneity which contemporary commen-

tators on the Revolution are painting, but it is required of
scholars that they look below the surface, and if they do
they may well find that in the Thirteen Colonies on the
eve of the Revolution the rich were getting richer while a
class of depressed and indigent persons was growing up.
Indubitably class feelings were quickening. One need
only point to the tenant rebellion of 1766 in New York's
Hudson Valley that was forcibly suppressed[26] and to the
Regulator movement on the North Carolina frontier, to
cite just two examples. And if anyone still wishes to
harbor the illusion that American society was a seamless
web, let him travel with William Byrd, as he surveyed the
boundary line dividing Virginia and North Carolina and
encountered in the swamps and wild lands a half-savage,
amoral amalgam of poor whites, Indians, and maroons, or
journey to the Carolina back country with the Rev.
Charles Woodmason, who reported a degree of sexual
grossness, criminality, and a general slackness of standards obtaining on the South Carolina frontier[27] that
might shock even a generation that has taken in stride
nuclear war, sexual deviation, and racial revolution.

In short, like so many historical oversimplifications, the
assumption that America skipped the feudal stage of history conveys an essential truth while ignoring or minimiz-
ing vestigial remnants of feudalism evident to a substantial degree in pre-Revolutionary America. The homogenized American landscape leaves no room on the canvas for
depicting the degree to which class favoritism persisted,
the extent of fraud in the administration of the land laws,
and the intensity of landlord-tenant conflicts, both in areas
where a manorial system was perpetuated and in regions
where tenancy was a technique of commercial farming.[28]
One cannot casually dismiss the land riots in New York
and New Jersey on the eve of the Revolution or the
survival of manorial obligations in parts of the former
province until the 1840's when the "tin horns and calico"

tenant rioting brought manorialism to an end. Nor can one lightly disregard the quitrent, that archaic survival as a commutation of feudal services which proved a constant and at times serious irritant, and was among the first feudal incidents to be abolished with the coming of the Revolution. These vestigial incidents only underscore the fact that, save perhaps in the Carolinas, there never was a comprehensive program to transplant feudalism to the Thirteen Colonies, nothing truly comparable to New France, although even in the latter country the attempt to tie the tenants to their labor obligations soon broke down.[29]

Landlordism was an issue on the eve of the American Revolution but hardly a precipitant of conflict between England and America, especially when one keeps in mind the topsy-turvy character of landlord-tenant politics. Where the landlords were Whigs and the tenants Tories, which was so often the case, the former were fighting to prevent the kind of land reform that the tenants felt they might expect should the royal government succeed in putting down the rebellion. In New York the Dutchess County tenants confidently expected that the King would "give them the Whigs' possessions."[30] In the early years of the Revolution William Smith, a suspected neutralist then under house arrest at Livingston Manor, reported that the Quaker Hill vicinity, where the tenant rioters of 1766 had made their last stand, stood forty to one "against Independency."[31] Because of the effectiveness of Tory propaganda promising that the tenants would get the estates of their Whig landlords, the Dutchess and Ulster Clintonians passed the word around that "when the Independency is established the manors would be parcelled out to such tenants as were in favor with the new established government."[32] Indeed, the tenancy counties of Revolutionary New York substantiate other evidence that the lower classes in some areas had a genuine economic interest in opposing a revolution led by the Whig élite, or, as Abraham Yates, Jr., put it some years later, "it is admitted that there are poor as well as rich Tories. Yet we know by experience that there would not have been a Tory in fifty in our late struggles if they had not been disaffected by the rich."[33]

The manor-rich Livingstons, whom their tenants denounced as "the robbers and murderers of common poor people," were filled with forebodings of a tenant rising to take over their properties. Warned that precisely that would happen should their tenants' impoverishment deepen,[34] the Livingstons soon found themselves fighting two wars, one against the British and another against their own tenants. The latter, denied perpetual leases, rose up in 1777 to join the British regulars, in expectation of fee simple holdings as a reward for their loyalty. The failure of the Burgoyne invasion soon stilled the menace of armed rebellion in the upstate manors, but as reluctant Whigs, the subdued tenants aligned themselves with their landlords' political opponents.

Another example of tranplanted feudalism is seen in the arrangements entered into by migrating Scottish tackmen, or agrarian middlemen, who farmed part of their tack and let the rest to undertenants. When the privileges of subletting were taken away from the tackmen in Scotland they conceived the idea of inducing their tenants to emigrate with them to America. "We shall carry a clan to America," one of the tackmen wrote, "and when they are there, they must work for us, or starve."[35] In New York the tackmen's tenants accepted the Toryism of their landlords, as did the quasi-feudal retainers of Sir John Johnson, and the followers of the Jessup brothers, Charlotte County lumber barons, and of Philip Skene, although the disaster which overcame Burgoyne made reluctant Patriots of many an upstate Tory tenant.[36] Observing that New York, the only colony with a large tenantry, was the least inclined to rebellion, the North Ministry in 1780 approved a plan to set up a new colony for the American Loyalists to be established between Nova Scotia and Massachusetts and to be known as "New Ireland." Frankly seeking to lay the "ground for an aristocratic power," the Ministry provided for leasing lands in large tracts rather than setting up small freehold estates.

In other states where Patriots were conspicuous as landlords they could scarcely be held up to their tenants as the embodiment of a root-and-branch reform of the land system. Take the case of the Patriot leader Richard Henry Lee of Virginia, who like other members of his family had a special talent for accumulating enemies. Lee carried on a feud with his tenants during the early years of the Revolution. When he proposed changing the payments due him under the leases from a money rental to payments in wheat or tobacco, he shrewdly protected himself against currency inflation but in so doing brought down upon his head the wrath of a number of his tenants.[37]

If, then, Revolutionary lines were not clearly drawn between landlord and tenant or big versus small landowner, it is because the landless and the yeoman farmer, whatever their Whig proclivities, did not view the Revolutionary leadership as being committed to a redistribution of land. In fact, from the available evidence one can make out an argument in reverse. It was the big speculators, not the little man, who opposed the royal land policy. Since the Crown land reforms of 1774 banned the large grant while promising protection to settlers by means of advertised auction sales, the people who reacted violently against the new land policy were speculators rather than potential settlers. True, Jefferson, in his *A Summary View*, saw fit to criticize the recent Crown terms set for purchase as restricting the populating of the country,[38] but one has to search the Declaration of Independence rather closely to discover land restriction as being enumerated among the wrongs charged to George III. This does not mean that land distribution was not consciously in the minds of some of the Patriot leaders. Thomas Jefferson, for one, considered the Revolutionary ferment as posing a challenge, even an opportunity, for broad social change. In each of Jefferson's three drafts of the Virginia Constitution of 1776 he proposed that fifty acres of unappropriated lands be distributed to "every person . . . neither owning nor having ever owned that quantity" of land, "and that no other person shall be capable of taking an appropriation."[39] We now know that Jefferson's good intentions, as exemplified in the Land Office Act of 1779, were exploited by speculators for purposes other than what he intended. This was the omnipresent danger, that despite the opening up of the Crown lands in the West, a vast domain snatched by the vigilant peacemakers of Paris in 1782, and despite the confiscation of immense Tory estates, predatory land speculators would engross the newly available lands instead of their being distributed to the landless or the small farmers. Himself a master hand at land speculation and engrossment, the knowledgeable Robert Morris pointed out to the Continental Congress in 1782 that "a large proportion of America is the property of great landholders," that "they monopolize it without cultivation," that for the most part they are "at no expense either of money or personal service to defend it," and that they impede both the settlement and the cultivation of the country by "keeping the price higher by monopoly than otherwise it would be."[40]

The totality of readily available evidence of land monopoly, of the acute stage which landlord-tenant controversies had reached, and of the presence of other sources of friction stemming from antifeudal or antimanorial trends serves to controvert the thesis that America did in fact skip the feudal age. At the same time it must be conceded in all candor that such feudal and manorial trappings as were transplanted were in the main rapidly transformed in America.

Those who would still argue the thesis that America's nonfeudal character was of central importance in explaining why the American Revolution was political and ideological rather than social implicitly accept the stereotype of a feudal society surviving in France during the death throes of the *ancien régime*. Yet they need hardly be reminded that modern researchers have conclusively controverted this stereotype. Louis XVI himself abolished feudalism on the royal domains, and by the eve of the French Revolution, as Georges Lefebvre has shown, the bourgeoisie probably owned as much rural land as did the nobility. In 1789 the great majority of French peasants had been free for many generations. Not only were most of the peasantry no longer serfs, but they were in fact landowners, holding about 30 percent of all the land of France. To the French peasant private property was as sacred as it was to an American freeholder. What differentiated France and America was the depth of class antagonism to the nobility existing in the former nation and largely absent in American society. As a result, Revolutionary America never witnessed the peasant rioting of the "July Days" in France. No American nobility existed to constitute the backbone of an émigré group. Lord Fairfax was the only British peer in 1775 permanently residing in any of the colonies. "Lord Stirling's" peerage was of dubious standing and he actually became a Patriot general. The two conspicuous baronets, Sir John Johnson in New York and Sir William Pepperell in Maine, became Loyalist exiles, it is true, but there were at least as many social leaders on the Whig as on the Tory side, and this was a real point of difference between the two revolutions.

One could wish for M. Lefebvre's simplistic class war approach, but it simply will not fit the pattern of the

American Revolution. Class feeling was strong, if not intense. Perhaps the Tories had more of it than the affluent Whigs, but both sides were conscious of and even concerned about the potential role of the lower class in the Revolutionary struggle. General Thomas Gage talked of "that insolent and infatuated mob," and various royal governors were alarmed at "the dastardly spirit of our common people," whom they castigated as "rabble." As early as 1775 the forthright and imprudent Rev. Jonathan Boucher noted a growing hostility between labor and employer.[41] An extreme Tory like the Rev. Samuel Peters of Connecticut viewed the Revolutionary party as "the Vulgars" and "ungovernable, righteous, and high-handed moberenes."[42] Another Tory, Jonathan Sewall of the Bay Colony, wrote: "Everything I see is laughable, cursable, and damnable; my pew in the church is covered into a pork tub; my house into a den of rebels, thieves and lice; my farm in possession of the very worst of all God's creation; my few debts all gone to the devil with my debtors." Then, with ill-concealed irony, he acknowledged that, as Dr. Pangloss viewed it, "all this is right . . . and this is the best of all possible worlds."[43] M'Fingal as a Tory jeered:

> While every clown that tills the plains,
> Though bankrupt in estate and brains,
> By this new light transformed to traitor,
> Forsakes his plough to turn dictator.

Now it is understandable that the highly placed Loyalists who formed the Old Establishment in America should hold the lower classes in contempt. What is significant, however, is that the more perceptive Tory leaders recognized elements of class struggle within the Patriot movement. Thomas Hutchinson, perhaps the best informed member of the Tory camp, while noting the control exercised in governmental affairs by the "rabble of the town of

Boston," pointed out that the mob was controlled in turn by "a superior set of master-masons and carpenters," and they, in turn, in matters of importance, were directed by the committee of merchants. To Hutchinson it was perfectly clear that the wealthy élite were exploiting discord for their own ends. How long could the affluent remain in the saddle? That was a question that puzzled the Tories and was of deep concern to some of the Whig élite. In New York the Tory-inclined William Smith noted the division among the Patriots between "the popular and the landed interest," and mordantly remarked that the latter were "losing their significance every day" and would "be happy if they can save their estates."[44]

In recognizing that the Whig élite shared with them a deep-rooted fear of the lower classes, the Tories demonstrated a degree of perception of social issues they normally lacked in political matters. The Patriot leaders did not conceal their concern lest their political revolution plunge the country into social upheaval. James Otis, onetime darling of the mob, might insist that absolute power "is *originally* and *ultimately* in the people," but when a group of radicals agitated for the reform of the Massachusetts government, he observed sneeringly in 1776, "When the pot boils, the scum will rise." Lawyer John Adams was dismayed at the attitude of debtors who rejoiced that the coming of the Revolution meant the closing of courts and the barring of creditors' collection machinery. "Such a levelling spirit prevails," he remarked to John Sullivan only a few weeks after Lexington and Concord, "even in. men called the first among mighty, that I fear we shall be obliged to call in a military force to do that which our civil government was originally designed for." Save in a few cases, as with the wild rioting against the Philadelphia speculators in the fall of '79, that extreme step proved unnecessary, but uneasiness continually swept the ranks of the affluent among the Patriots. In Charleston the head of the Sons of Liberty, the radical Christopher Gadsden, came to fear the hasty and frequent "meetings of the liberty tree." Is this "not a disease among us," he asked in 1778, "far more dangerous than anything that can arise from the whole herd of contemptible, exportable Tories?"[45] During the financial crisis of 1779–80, when a popular demand arose for stern price controls and the confiscation of Tory estates, the mother of Robert R. Livingston prayed for "peace and independence and deliverance from the persecutions of the lower classes who I forsee will be as despotic as any prince (if not more so) in Europe."[46] In short, it would be easy to document the assertion that the Whig leadership were almost as much concerned about the dangers from leveling forces as they were about the perils of subversion, disloyalty, and treason, that they had a pessimistic view of human nature, and that their debt to Hobbes was almost as great as it was to Locke.

It is perhaps paradoxical that the American War for Independence, while containing elements of both a social and a political revolution, failed to align social classes in a clear-cut manner for or against independence. Instead, the divided allegiance of the lower classes converts the American Revolution into a classic example of a civil war. As one Connecticut Tory expressed it, "Nabour was against Nabour, Father against Son and the son against the Father, and he that would not thrust his one blaid through his brothers heart was cald an Infimous fillon."[47] But the civil war was hardly confined to the lower class. Consider the cases of Benjamin Franklin and his natural son William, New Jersey's Royalist governor, as leaders of opposing sides, of John Jay and his meddlesome neutralist brother Sir James, of Gouverneur Morris and his Tory mother, or the divided Lovell family, along with so many other examples of tragic cleavages among the families of the Patriot leadership.

Those who look upon the civil war in America during the Revolution as a decorous affair in contrast with the Terror during the French Revolution and the slaughter of the Communards in Paris in 1871, should have spent a winter belowground in a Connecticut mine, or suffered the filth, infection, and depravity of a British prison ship in the East River, or been scalped by Tory rangers and their Indian allies on the New York and Pennsylvania frontier, or been caught in that internecine struggle waged in the South with almost unexampled ferocity. There rugged bands of irregulars looting Tory women of their jewels gave a class overtone to the civil war, albeit there was plunder aplenty on the Tory side and on the part of Redcoats and Hessians. In a war so fiercely waged it was perhaps natural that the Tory rangers should seem more vindictive than the Redcoats, who had no obvious stake in the struggle, and that the Patriots were much less inclined to forgive their Loyalist compatriots than they were the professional armies that had been shipped across the wide Atlantic to suppress their liberties.

The war brought hardship and impoverishment to people of all classes. "You can have no idea of the sufferings of many who from affluence are reduced to the most abject poverty, and others who die in obscurity," wrote Margaret Beekman Livingston to John Jay months after Yorktown.[48] Still the fact that the lower classes could be found on both sides of the struggle prevents our categorizing the American Revolution as a class war. The majority of the Massachusetts Loyalists may have been of prosperous and upper-class families, but that did not prevent Dorcas Griffiths, a notorious prostitute, from joining their company and becoming a Tory claimant. In New York the upstate levelers were generally Tories and there was a heavy vein of Toryism in the Regulator country even though Tories may never have numbered a clear-cut numerical majority of that group.[49] Loyalists were heavily recruited from the ranks of the more recent emigrants, regardless of social position, and from cultural minorities like the Sandemanian sect or the Baptists in Massachusetts.[50]

In making a head count of muster rolls one caution should be borne in mind. Despite their predilection for one side or the other, the lower classes often had little free choice. The tenant farmers of Dutchess County who opposed the break with England were left with the cruel alternative of joining the Patriot militia or running away, as the Redcoats never exercised effective control in that area. Contrariwise, in the environs of New York City the British were not above forcible recruiting of those who refused to volunteer for the King's service.[51] In the Carolina back country many people tried desperately to avoid taking loyalty oaths and only served in the militia under compulsion. Some, like Alexander Chesney and the opportunistic Moses Kirkland, bore arms against the Crown but switched sides when the first opportunity arose. Service in the Revolutionary militia, in short, is at best prima facie evidence of loyalty, which may be rebutted by other testimony.[52]

Take the Regulator movement in North Carolina as a case in point. The unrest in that distressed area points the direction that social revolutionary ferment in America could take. A section comprised largely of newly arrived emigrants, with very shallow roots in the American soil, its spokesmen sought such reforms as a written ballot, proportional taxation, paper money to be kept in permanent circulation, land reform to prevent monopoly, and the trial of all suits for debt above 40 shillings and under £10 without lawyers and before a jury of six freeholders.[53] Still, it is a continuing matter of controversy as to which side the Regulators took in the Revolutionary struggle, once their movement had been crushed at the Alamance. Governor Martin presumed that a petition from the back country signed by over five hundred persons professing loyalty to the King and hostility to the "most profligate and abandoned Republican faction,"[54] had come from the Regulators. At his request a royal pardon was granted, excepting only Hermon Husband, who became a refugee Whig. But if the Regulators had Loyalist intentions it is certainly not clear that they stayed on the Tory side. The uncommitted and the neutralists, along with the faint of heart, felt let down by the succession of British military defeats, by the fact that the forays the Redcoats made into the interior were invariably followed by withdrawals which exposed their Tory supporters to the full ferocity of their vindictive countrymen.[55] The presence of a name on the roster of Revolutionary troops, particularly of the militia, is of itself no proof of a Patriotic disposition. One investigator has made a head count which gives the Whig Regulators a decided edge over the Tory Regulators, but such a conclusion ignores the absence of available alternatives and the pressures of coercion and conformity. Considering the "unremitting pressure" exerted upon the Tories, it is little wonder, so James Simpson informed Lord George Germain, that "some of them had found means to make their peace."

In probing the American Revolutionary social structure for evidence of class conflict it would be unrealistic to confine our investigation to the free white population. One simply must come to grips with the fascinating problem posed by those vast numbers, both white and Negro, who were held in bondage. First of all, it should be borne in mind that by the eve of the Revolution the number of white servants held by indenture for limited terms exceeded the totals for any other period in colonial history. The swollen rolls of white servitude came largely as the consequence of that rising wave of immigration to the mainland of North America, since so heavy a proportion of immigrants came over as redemptioners bound to work off their passage. The traffic in white convict servants seems also to have been at its height at this time, and the number of debtors who were sold into servitude by court order to satisfy their judgment creditors was steady if not increasing.[56] Save in cases of bound servants gaining their freedom by enlistment, often over the vehement protests of their masters, the Revolution did nothing to end and little to ameliorate the practice of white bondage. In fact, the evidence is at best mixed as to the proportion of redemptioners who achieved a stake in colonial society as against the failures and the dropouts.[57]

How Patriot employers may have felt about the Revolutionary fervor of their employees is suggested by a memorial drawn up in May, 1777, by a Cumberland, Pennsylvania, County Committee opposing the enlistment of servants without the consent of their masters because "all Apprentices and servants are the Property of their masters and mistresses, and every mode of depriving such masters and mistresses of their Property is a Violation of the Rights of mankind, contrary to the . . . Continental Congress, and an offence against the Peace of the good People of this State."[58] True, the redemptioner traffic ceased during the war years, but it enjoyed a new lease on life at war's end. In January, 1784, a meeting of New York citizens denounced "the traffic of white people" as contrary "to the idea of liberty this country so happily established."[59] Time, massive emigration into the American labor market, and the gradual enactment of bankruptcy laws and laws ending imprisonment for debt would within another generation implement, so far as the white workers were concerned, the notions of freedom and equality to which Jefferson had given so eloquent expression.

At least it can be said for white bondage that it constituted merely a temporary status. Freedom may have been the ultimate prospect for all whites, but certainly not for most Negroes. Indeed, Negro slavery darkened the Revolutionary skies as a great, brooding omnipresence. Its magnitude and pervasive role stands as a mocking reminder of the unreality of that composite portrait that depicts Revolutionary society as homogeneous if not homogenized. Here was a system seemingly adapted to fit the labor conditions of the New World, yet providing class contrasts far more startling and a degree of social stratification far more rigid than anything that could be found in the England of George III, the France of Louis XVI, or the Spain of Charles III, nations not then renowned for social equality.

With the enunciation of the Great Declaration the die was cast. Would a revolution overtly dedicated to the principle of equality end this greatest of all inequalities? Some Southerners felt that a solution must be found. Some, like Patrick Henry, continued to hold slaves because of "the general inconvenience of living without them," while looking forward to the day when "this lamentable evil" would be abolished.[60] Jefferson left no stone unturned to mitigate the evil. He tried unsuccessfully to write into the Virginia Constitution of 1776 a provision providing that "no person hereafter coming into the state would be held in slavery,"[61] and his inclusion of the slave trade in the list of evils ascribed to George III in the Declaration of Independence was stricken out by his fellow delegates.[62] The man who trembled for his country when he remembered that God was just,[63] later sought to bar slavery from all the territories, and had his advice been followed this nation might have been spared a bloody civil war.

Hardly a month after John Hancock had affixed his bold signature to a noble Declaration, a colorful and contentious planter and ex-slave trader, the Patriot Henry Laurens, in a letter to his son asserted his readiness to apply the ideals of the Declaration to the bondsmen on his estates. He planned to manumit them, even though he was opposed by "great powers," as he expressed it, "the laws and customs of my country, my own and the avarice of my countrymen." Laurens denied that he was "one of those who dare trust in Providence for defence and security of their own liberty while they enslave and wish to continue in slavery thousands who are as well entitled to freedom as themselves."[64]

Although such egalitarian sentiments were voiced by a few choice and generous spirits among slave-owning Southerners, it is ironical that no single event did more to propel the uncommitted Southern planters into the camp of rebellion than Lord Dunmore's call summoning the Negro slaves to the British cause with a promise of freedom. An "infamous proclamation," Robert Carter Nicholas might thunder, but slaves escaped in droves to the British lines to rally under the banner of Virginia's royal governor, whom Virginia's Patriots contemptuously denominated "our African Hero." In issuing its call for independence the Virginia Convention denounced its governor for "carrying on a piratical and savage war against us, tempting our slaves by every artifice to resort to him, and training and employing them against their masters."[65]

Nor was the Patriot South alone in taking military action to forestall a Negro uprising. Up in Goshen, New York, a special guard was raised having as its declared purpose the "maintaining the internal peace of the Township of Goshen" and "preventing the insurrection of Tories, prisoners, slaves, etc."[66] From such isolated military measures one should not infer that the North was sympathetic to slavery. Quite the contrary. In addition to Vermont, five of the original Thirteen States initiated programs of emancipation before the Federal Convention of 1787, and two others followed soon thereafter. Most of these steps affected relatively few slaves, especially during the war years. In sum, Northern antislavery sentiment, buttressed in the Congress by the words and deeds of enlightened Southerners, was not mobilized quickly enough to prove a decisive factor in the contest for the loyalty of the Negro in the Revolution.

The enormous number of slaves deserting or being evacuated by the British forces to safe areas created a topsy-turvy situation, in which the forces fighting under the standard of liberty did not command the affection or allegiance of a substantial segment of the Negro people. True, free Negroes volunteered for the Patriot army,[67] and large numbers served in labor battalions. Granted, too, that a few farsighted Patriots like Alexander Hamilton and his friend Colonel John Laurens urged the raising of a number of Negro battalions, "to give them freedom with their swords," as Hamilton put it.[68] Generally, however, the Negroes were feared rather than embraced. As one Whig in a Crèvecoeur sketch remarked to a Negro boy, "They say you are a good fellow, only a little Tory-fied like most of your colour."[69] Significantly, Benjamin West's painting of the Loyalists being welcomed to England in 1783 by Britannia includes an emancipated Negro family and an Indian chief.

Somebody might make out a plausible argument that the British fought to free the slaves and the Americans fought to keep them enslaved. The preamble of South Carolina's Constitution of 1776 would be Exhibit No. 1. There is something a little incongruous about a portrayal of the American Revolution in terms of class polarity when states like the Carolinas and Georgia, obsessed with the specter of slave insurrections,[70] preferred to let their country be overrun by the Redcoats rather than comply with the urgent recommendations of Congress to permit the enrollment of Negroes in the American army. The concept of the Revolution as a war for freedom and equality hardly jibes with the scheme that General

Thomas Sumter put into effect for paying his troops. Under "Sumter's Law" he paid his soldiers with slaves plundered from the Tories, setting a pay scale ranging from 3½ slaves per annum for a colonel to a fully grown slave for a private for each month's enlistment.[71] Although it is to Francis Marion's credit that he denounced the Gamecock's proposal as inhumane, unmoral, and violative of due process, it received the cautious sanction of Quaker Nathanael Greene.[72]

What an ironic twist could have been given to the Declaration of Independence had the North Ministry been clever enough to turn the war into an antislavery crusade! The English religious leader John Wesley grasped the issue better than the Whig liberals. "The Negroes in America are slaves, the whites enjoy liberty," he declared. "Is not then all this outcry about Liberty and Slavery mere rant, and playing upon words?"[73] Fortunate for America's libertarian traditions, even had the North Ministry the wit to conceive so masterly a stroke of propaganda, British slave-trading interests, the West Indian sugar planters, and the desperate hope of winning the Lower South back to the Crown would have conspired to frustrate so bold a design. It is significant, nonetheless, that when the war ended, whether out of vindictiveness, reprisal, or for humanitarian reasons,[74] the British occupation forces refused to repatriate the refugee slaves and turn them over to their Patriot masters. It might be added parenthetically that the numbers evacuated may have at least equaled the total of white Tories who fled America. It is also significant that John Jay, long committed to antislavery, declined for reasons principally of morality to press the planters' case for indemnification of their slave property when this issue came up in his negotiations with Lord Grenville in 1794.

In November, 1925, the respected American historical scholar J. Franklin Jameson gave a number of lectures which he felicitously entitled *The American Revolution Considered as a Social Movement*. Coming at the flood-tide of the economic determinists and quasi-Marxist writers on the American past, Jameson's seminal lectures enjoyed a great vogue for several decades. It could hardly be denied that so cataclysmic an event as the American Revolution would be bound to effect significant social changes, to bring new men forward, and to provide a forum for new ideas that may have been denied hitherto. Jameson said many sensible things, but it is now fashionable to exaggerate his thesis in order to decapitate a straw man. For the neo-conservatives who find equality already established, the American Revolution did not create the baby. It merely took off a few of the wrappings. To this new school the most remarkable fact about the American Revolution was not that social change took place but rather that it was held within such relatively modest bounds.[75]

Let us consider a few of the major areas treated by Dr. Jameson. Take the confiscation of Tory estates, prime example cited by those who see the War for Independence as a social revolution analogous to the French Revolution. True, the parallelism is striking, but the social leveling in either case has perhaps been distorted. In America the purpose of these confiscatory measures was not to create a peasant freeholding class but to punish outstanding nonconformists and to raise funds desperately needed to carry on the war. In Virginia, with few exceptions, the property sold belonged to persons whose actual residence was in England, and most of the prominent Tory families remained in undisturbed possession of their estates.[76] Thus, while the great nonjuring landowner, Lord Fairfax, was unmolested by the Virginia Assembly, his heirs who were Englishmen were less fortunate. The parallelism to the French Revolution is striking. In France the only lands confiscated were those of the Church, the émigrés, and persons condemned for political offenses, and, as in America, the Revolution posed no threat to the property of the nobility who stayed in France and remained peaceable.[77] In some respects the French Revolution was less radical in its early phases than the American. For example, the National Assembly provided compensation for the abolition of substantial feudal dues in contrast to the uncompensated confiscation of Tory estates and the abolition of quitrents in America. Only in the radical phase of the French Revolution in 1793 was such compensation stopped.

In both revolutions the confiscated lands were sold to the highest bidder, not given away, and in each the initial purpose of the forfeitures was fiscal rather than social. The French peasants acquired the church lands through middlemen very much the way small farmers in the American states eventually secured Loyalist lands by purchasing them from speculators, but because of the limited amount of land previously available in France, the results of the redistribution of the confiscated lands were more egalitarian and liberative in France than in America, where so much other land, vastly greater in extent than in France, was opened up for settlement by the peace.

Furthermore, the pattern of distribution of Tory lands varies from colony to colony and from county to county. In New York City and Annapolis expensive urban properties were acquired by speculators and wealthy investors. Contrariwise, in rural Dutchess County, New York, and on Phillipsburgh Manor, as well as in Frederick County, Maryland, manor tenants exercised pre-emption rights and became freeholders as a result of confiscations.[78] Small landowners in New Jersey's Somerset County found extreme difficulty in picking up forfeited estates, as confiscations often proved a windfall to wealthy insiders. Not only that, but when estates were broken up they often went to enlarge the holdings of adjacent farmers, thus leading to a concentration rather than to a breakup of holdings. The subject is indeed complex and deserves a precise county-by-county investigation before any valid generalizations can be drawn about what seemed on paper to have the broadest social implications of any of the revolutionary measures adopted by the American Patriots. To date, if one must must generalize, the evidence suggests that rural holdings were extensively subdivided, urban properties went from the affluent of one camp to those of the other.

In short, before we dismiss the notion that land confiscation in America had any egalitarian base we must distinguish the grounds upon which the Patriots sought to justify the confiscation of Loyalist private property from those upon which the Revolutionary leaders stood in proposing to take over the great public lands of the proprietors. As one correspondent reminded Lady Juliana Penn in the summer of 1782, any proposals in the peace negotiations to restore Loyalist estates would not apply to the proprietary lands. "It was taken from the Proprietarys, not in a way of confiscation," this commentator pointed out, "but upon principle of policy and expedience." "They thought the estate two [sic] large for a subject to possess, supposing it dangerous to the public that so much property should rest in the hands of one family."[79]

Jameson has in recent years been criticized for giving undue weight to the democratic effects of the abolition of entails and primogeniture. Diggers in county courthouses have shown that, although there were some large estates held in entail, like the bulk of the estate of Thomas, sixth Lord Fairfax of Cameron, these liberative moves did not affect a social revolution overnight, as most Southern planters made ample provision in their wills for the younger children in their families and a number of legal devices for breaking entails were already in wide use.[80] Indeed, if one stops to compare large landholdings in the South during the age when entail and primogeniture were in operation with the national period, when partible descent prevailed, one soon discovers that the later period saw a much more extensive consolidation of landholdings than had characterized pre-Revolutionary times, attesting to the far greater social leverage exerted by economics and technology than by the laws on the statute books.

Nevertheless, if entails and primogeniture were so inconsequential in pre-Revolutionary Virginia as Jameson's recent critics insist, one must wonder why so well-informed a lawyer as Thomas Jefferson was so concerned about the problem. The answer is that entails were a clot, stopping free circulation of land, whose liquidity was desperately needed by a heavily indebted planter class. Furthermore, entailments set a poor example for the egalitarian society that Jefferson himself envisioned. True, an entail could be docked by a private legislative act, but the process was costly, the enactment had to be approved by the Privy Council in England, and the proper people abroad had to be taken care of to ensure that the act of entailment would not be disallowed.[81] True, too, smaller entails, those under £200, might be broken by a writ of *ad quod damnum* from the Secretary's office,[82] but our concern is with land concentration, a threat not posed by smaller holdings.

Jefferson properly considered a reform of the real property laws as central to a reform of a society, whose egalitarianism was land-structured. As he interpreted English legal history, the introduction of feudalism into England by the Normans brought about a system of inequality that was not suited to those who migrated to America, persons who, as he put it, "were laborers, not lawyers." In order to make sure that the undistributed land was considered as belonging to all the people, he advocated legislation striking at feudalism by making land allodial and providing that the unappropriated land be sold in small parcels for the benefit of the commonwealth and to the advantage of the new settlers who would be going into the Western country.

If, then, primogeniture and entails were already on their way out, their abolition in the decade following the Revolution reflects not only the past experience of the colonists but the measured judgment of the Revolutionary state governments that the legal devices for the descent and distribution of land must, so far as possible, guarantee and perpetuate an egalitarian society. England, we might do well to remember, waited until 1925 to pass the Real Property Act and thereby to reach the point to which Jefferson had already brought Virginia by 1776. That gap of one hundred and fifty years represents the difference between a society that achieved democracy by a revolutionary process and one that reached it by glacial stages. Despite the toll of deeds and wills that some indefatigable researchers have carried on, Jefferson, out of a concern for supplanting "an aristocracy of wealth" by "an aristocracy of virtue and talent," expressed both in his reform of the land law and in his radical proposals for public education, struck a symbolic blow against a class-structured society.

The liberative or upgrading effect of the wiping out of debts owed by Southern planters, notably Virginians, to English and Scottish merchants received much more attention in the post-Revolutionary period than at the hands of recent historians. The evidence of indebtedness is massive, and the devices employed to avoid payment provide some of the strongest arguments for considering the War for Independence a social revolution.[83] There was, to be sure, some justice in the sneers the Irish poet Tom Moore aimed at

> Those vaunted demagogues who nobly rose
> From England's debtors to be England's foes,
> Who could their monarch in their purse forget
> And break allegiance but to cancel debt.

Hardly had the war gotten under way than an act was rushed through the Virginia legislature authorizing the payment into the state loan office of debts due British

subjects from citizens of Virginia, such payments to constitute a discharge of the debtor from all further obligations to his creditor.[84] When news reached America that
the Treaty of Peace provided that creditors on either side
should meet with no lawful impediment to the recovery in
full value of their debts, there was a furor in Virginia.
George Mason wrote Patrick Henry that the question was
frequently raised in conversation: "If we are now to pay
the debts due to the British merchants, *what have we
been fighting for all this while?*"[85]

In the post-Revolutionary period Patrick Henry as
spokesman for the debtor group brought about the defeat
in the Virginia Assembly of a bill for compliance with a
Congressional resolution calling upon the states to repeal
all laws repugnant to the treaty. Finally, when such a bill
was passed a provision was added that it would not go
into effect until Great Britain had evacuated the posts and
paid for the slaves.[86] As Isaac Harrell has pointed out, a
majority of the debtors in Virginia had neither the means
nor the inclination to fulfill the debt provisions of the
peace treaty. Since a substantial part of the debt was
ultimately collected, due in no small part to the strong
stand of John Jay, both in his capacity as Chief Justice
and as the American negotiator of the treaty bearing his
name, the planter class at best gained precious time, but,
in the end, was at least as much impoverished, if not more
so, than when the war began. How strongly Virginians
felt about paying these debts is revealed by a Grand Jury
of the Federal Circuit of Virginia, which, in August, 1794,
presented "as a *national* grievance the recovery of debts
due to British subjects."

John Adams, who was to become fully cognizant of the
prominent role played by the issue of the Virginia debts in
the councils of the nation, was also appreciative of the fact
that Northern debtors, as well as Southern, were com-
forted by the breakdown of debt collection machinery in-

cident to the coming of the Revolution. "Is this the object for which I have been contending?" Adams asked himself with righteous indignation.[87]

Whether or not some individuals fought the Revolution to get out of debt or to acquire someone else's land, most of the people on the Patriot side had certain common objectives. In order to clarify the purposes for which the war was fought we need to distinguish between the great reforms which stemmed *directly* from the Revolution and those which were incidents of the Revolution even though an integral part of it. The former were political in character: the concept of government resting upon the consent of the people, constitution making, and republican institutions. These were truly revolutionary notions and the War for Independence firmly fixed them upon our frame of government. The latter were social and economic, and certainly not part of the avowed objectives of the war.

An analogy might fairly be drawn to the First World War. Perhaps the greatest change which came in the wake of that conflict, so far as America was concerned, was the emancipation of American women, an extraordinary phenomenon which liberated women from the home and thrust them into the factory. The revolutionary impact of this social upheaval on postwar life, politics, marriage, morals, and the family is incalculable. And it never would have happened so fast had it not been for the manpower shortage resultant upon World War I. But we have usually been taught that we went to war with Germany over her renewal of unrestricted submarine warfare or because the House of Morgan had floated loans to the Allies. Most readers would be surprised to hear that when President Wilson called upon Congress to declare war he really intended to free American womanhood from the shackles of housework. Now, within certain limitations, the analogy to the American Revolution is an eminently fair one. We did not declare our independence of George III in order to reform the land laws, change the criminal codes, spread popular education, or separate church and state. We broke with England to achieve political independence, freedom from external controls, emancipation, if you will, of the bourgeoisie from mercantilist restraints, but in the process of achieving those goals we had aroused expectations, encouraged aspirations, and created a climate conducive to a measurable degree of social reform.

All in all, revolutions are a very complex subject, not least of all the American Revolution. One can never predict the turnings they will take. When Washington assumed command of the army in Cambridge, he wrote his brother: "I am embarked on a wide ocean, boundless in its prospect and from whence perhaps no safe harbor is to be found." If in its origins and common purpose the American Revolution was an anticolonial war fought for independence and national identity, it was also marked by liberative currents, class conflicts, and egalitarian urges. A monolithic interpretation of the Revolution as a purely political movement will not explain many things that happened in the course of that conflict. Clearly there is something more to the Spirit of '76 than "Redcoats go home"! There was talk about equality. There was talk about "the pursuit of happiness." And some people were determined that, in addition to independence from British rule, these goals should be realized.

A seven-year struggle for political independence overlapped in time an ambitious campaign for social reforms that may be considered to have been initiated before the inception of the Revolution and to have continued long after its conclusion. Benjamin Rush candidly perceived the dual nature of that great struggle. In his Fourth of July Address at Philadelphia in 1787 he observed: "There is nothing more common than to confound the terms American Revolution with those of the late American War. The American War is over, but this is far from being the case with the American Revolution. On the contrary but the first act of the great drama is closed."[88] It is this understanding of the dual character of the War for Independence which makes the American Revolution not an event in American history alone but a turning point in world history, not a single crisis settled in a brief span of years but a broad movement of liberation which has not yet run its course.

NOTES TO CHAPTER II

1. Robert Palmer, *The Age of the Democratic Revolution* (Princeton, 1959–64), II, 574.

2. Hannah Arendt, *On Revolutions,* p. 87.

3. Richard Buel, Jr., "Democracy and the American Revolution: A Frame of Reference," *William and Mary Quarterly,* XXI (1964), 165 *et seq.*

4. See J. R. Hollingsworth, "Consensus and Continuity in Recent American Historical Writing," *South Atlantic Quarterly,* LXI (1962), 40 *et seq.*

5. Arendt, *op. cit.,* pp. 54, 55.

6. *Ibid.,* p. 87. On the issue of hunger one might well contrast Albert Mathiez, *The French Revolution,* translated by Catherine A. Phillips (New York, 1928), and C. E. Labrousse, *La crise de l'économie française à la fin de l'Ancien Régime et au début de la Revolution* (2 vols. in 1, Paris, 1943).

7. See J. L. Talmon, *The Origins of Totalitarian Democracy* (London, 1955).

8. Georges Lefebvre, *The Coming of the French Revolution* (New York, 1960).

9. *View of Causes and Consequences of the American Revolution* (London, 1797), pp. lxvii–lxxxiii.

10. For example, Carl Bridenbaugh (*Cities in Revolt* [New York, 1955], p. 291) attributes the Revolution to the frustration of the middle class.

11. *The Anatomy of Revolution* (New York, 1957), pp. 101, 102.

12. L. A. Harper, "The Effect of the Navigation Acts on the Thirteen Colonies," in R. B. Morris, ed., *The Era of the American Revolution* (New York, 1939), pp. 3–39.

13. Barbé-Marbois to Vergennes, Mass. Hist. Soc. *Proceed-*

ings, VII, 262-266; E. B. Greene, *The Revolutionary Genera-tion, 1763–1790* (New York, 1943), pp. 330–360; Clarence Ver Steeg, "The American Revolution Considered as an Economic Movement," *Huntington Library Quarterly*, XX (1956–57), 361–372.

14. Force, *Amer. Arch.*, 4th ser., II, 959–960.

15. R. B. Morris, "Insurrection in Massachusetts," in Daniel Aaron, *America in Crisis* (New York, 1952), p. 21.

16. Elisha Douglas, *Rebels and Democrats* (Chapel Hill, 1955), p. 146.

17. See the perceptive article by Darline Shapiro, "Ethan Allen: Philosopher-Theologian," *William and Mary Quarterly*, XXI (1964), 236–255.

18. See Robert Palmer, *The Age of the Democratic Revolu-tion* (Princeton, 1959), I, 188.

19. Louis Hartz, *The Liberal Tradition in America* (New York, 1955), pp. 5, 6.

20. D. J. Boorstin, *Genius of American Politics*, Chap. I.

21. *Jefferson Papers* (Boyd ed.), I, 478.

22. C. S. Grant, *Democracy in the Connecticut Frontier Town of Kent* (New York, 1961), pp. 170–172.

23. R. E. and B. K. Brown, *Virginia, 1705–1786: Democracy or Aristocracy* (East Lansing, Mich., 1964).

24. Aubrey C. Land, "Economic Base and Social Structure: The Northern Chesapeake in the Eighteenth Century," *Journal of Economic History*, XXV (1965), 639–654.

25. Jackson Turner Main, *The Social Structure of Revolu-tionary America* (Princeton, 1965). For Philadelphia, see also the thesis paper of Alice H. Jones, "Personal Wealth, Its Size, Character and Distribution in Philadelphia and Rural Counties in Pennsylvania, New Jersey, and Delaware in 1774" (Wash-ington University, St. Louis, Mo.).

26. See Irving Mark, *Agrarian Conflicts in Colonial New York, 1711–1775* (New York, 1940).

27. See also remonstrance and petition of the South Caro-lina back country, Nov. 7, 1767, in Richard J. Hooker, ed., *The Carolina Back-Country on the Eve of the Revolution: The Journal and other Writings of Charles Woodmason, Anglican Itinerant* (Chapel Hill, N.C., 1953), pp. 213–233.

28. See L. C. Gray, *History of Agriculture in the Southern United States,* I, 386–391.

29. Sigmund Diamond, "An Experiment in Feudalism," *William and Mary Quarterly,* XVIII (1961), 2–34.

30. Samuel Dodge to the President of the New York Provincial Congress, *Journals of the Provincial Congress* (Albany, 1842), II, 106.

31. William Smith, *Historical Memoirs,* ed. by W. H. Sabine (New York, 1956–1958), II, 118. See also Staughton Lynd, *Anti-Federalism in Dutchess County, New York* (Chicago, 1962), Chap. IV, and "The Tenant Rising at Livingston Manor," May, 1777, *New York Hist. Soc. Qly.,* XLVIII (1964), 163–177; Patricia Joan Gordon, "Kinship and Class: The Livingstons of New York, 1675–1860" (doctoral dissertation, Columbia University, 1959).

32. Smith, *Hist. Memoirs,* II, 326.

33. "Essays on political subjects," by "Rough Hewer" (1788), Abraham Yates Papers, New York Public Library.

34. Thomas Tillotson to Robert R. Livingston, June, 1782—Robert R. Livingston Papers, New York Hist. Society. See also Smith, *Hist. Memoirs,* II, 392; George Dangerfield, *Chancellor Robert R. Livingston of New York, 1746–1813* (New York, 1960), pp. 20, 450.

35. Letter from "Veritas" to the *Edinburgh Advertiser,* Dec. 31, 1772, reprinted in *Scots Magazine,* XXXIV (1772), 697–700, cited by I. C. C. Graham, *Colonists from Scotland* (Ithaca, N.Y., 1956), p. 72, and developed by Margaret I. Adam, "The Highland Emigration of 1770," *Scottish Historical Review,* XVI (1918–19), 280–293.

36. Lansdowne Papers 66: 513–528—W. L. Clements Library; John T. Waugh, "The United Empire Loyalists," *Univ. of Buffalo Studies,* IV, No. 3 (Buffalo, 1925), 73–123. See also Eugene R. Fingerhut, "They Came Last: Immigrants from Great Britain to the Frontier of New York in the Revolutionary Period" (Ph.D. dissertation, Columbia University).

37. L. C. Ballagh, ed., *Letters of Richard Henry Lee* (2 vols., New York, 1911–1914), I, 298–301, 336–337.

38. *Jefferson Papers,* ed. by J. P. Boyd, I, 133. See also his Resolution on Land Grants, Mar. 27, 1775. *Ibid.,* p. 162.

39. *Ibid.*, pp. 344, 352, 362.

40. *Journals of the Continental Congress, 1774–1789,* XX, 429–447 (July 29, 1782).

41. *A View of the Causes and Consequences of the American Revolution* (London, 1797), p. 309.

42. O. Zeichner, *Connecticut's Years of Controversy* (Chapel Hill, N.C., 1950), p. 227.

43. "Letters of Jonathan Sewall," Mass. Hist. Soc. *Proceedings,* 2nd ser., X (January, 1896), 414.

44. *Historical Memoirs,* II, 280, 306.

45. Richard Walsh, *Charleston's Sons of Liberty: A Study of the Artisans, 1763–1789* (Columbia, S.C., 1959), p. 87.

46. Margaret Beekman Livingston to Robert R. Livingston, Dec. 30, 1779—Robert R. Livingston Papers, New York Hist. Soc.

47. Petition of Stephen Gorham, July 22, 1777, Fairfield Superior Court Papers, 1770–1779, Connecticut State Library, quoted by Zeichner, *Connecticut's Years of Controversy,* p. 235.

48. Claremont, April 21, 1782. Jay Papers, Columbia University Libraries.

49. Wallace Brown, *The King's Friends* (Providence, R.I., 1966), p. 30; Elmer D. Johnson, "The War of the Regulation: Its Place in History" (Ph.D. dissertation, Univ. of North Carolina); Robert W. Barnwell, "Loyalism in South Carolina, 1765–1785" (Ph.D. dissertation, Duke University).

50. See William H. Nelson, *The American Tory* (Oxford, 1962), p. 89. That the Loyalists recruited many from the ranks of the poor is borne out in Catherine S. Crary, "The Humble Immigrant and the American Dream: Some Case Histories, 1764–1775," *Mississippi Valley Hist. Rev.,* XLVI (1959), 46–66.

51. *Minutes of the Commissioners for Detecting and Defeating Conspiracies in the State of New York* (3 vols., Albany, 1909), I, 135.

52. Richard M. Brown, *The South Carolina Regulators* (Cambridge, Mass., 1963), pp. 129–130.

53. Petition of Inhabitants of Anson County, *North Carolina Colonial Records,* VIII, 75–78.

54. *Ibid.*, IX, 1162.

55. Alan S. Brown, ed., "James Simpson's Reports on the Carolina Loyalists, 1779–1780," *Journal of Southern History*, XXXL (1955), 513–515. For Tories switching sides, see C. S. Crary, "Humble Immigrant," *loc. cit.*, p. 60, and Loyalist Commission of Enquiry, Audit Office transcripts, New York Public Library.

56. See Richard B. Morris, *Government and Labor in Early America* (New York, 1946).

57. See *ibid.*, pp. 293–294; also A. E. Smith, *Colonists in Bondage* (Chapel Hill, N.C., 1947), pp. 299–300, and Columbia University Master's Essays by Margaret Cowden, "Lost Americans: On the Trail of Some New York Indentured Servants," and Eugene R. Fingerhut, "Immigrants in Colonial New York, 1770–1775."

58. *Pennsylvania Archives*, 1st ser., V, 340.

59. *Independent Journal* (New York), Jan. 24, 1784.

60. Patrick Henry to Anthony Benezet, Feb. 22, 1774, *William and Mary Quarterly*, 2nd ser., I (1921), 107–109.

61. *Jefferson Papers* (Boyd ed.), I, 353.

62. Dumas Malone, *Jefferson the Virginian* (Boston, 1948), p. 141.

63. Jefferson, *Notes on the State of Virginia* (Baltimore, 1800), p. 241.

64. See R. B. Morris, ed., *A Letter from Henry Laurens to His Son John Laurens, August 14, 1776* (New York, 1964).

65. See *Jefferson Papers*, I, 257, 266, 267, 290, 390, 471, 476, 477; Benjamin Quarles, *The Negro in the American Revolution* (Chapel Hill, 1961), pp. 111–157.

66. New York Hist. Soc., *Coll.*, 1915, II, 492.

67. Estimates will be found in George H. Moore, "Historical Notes on the Employment of Negroes in the American Army of the Revolution," *Magazine of History, with Notes and Queries*, No. 1 (1907).

68. R. B. Morris, ed., *Alexander Hamilton and the Founding of the Nation* (New York, 1957), p. 455.

69. Hector St. Jean de Crèvecoeur, *Sketches of Eighteenth Century America* (London, 1925), p. 310. See also C. M. and E. Andrews, *Journal of a Lady of Quality* (New Haven, 1921), pp. 200–201, for an account of armed whites patrolling and

searching for Negroes around Wilmington, N.C., who had taken to the woods.

70. See *Extract from the Journal of the Provincial Congresses of South Carolina, 1775–76* (Columbia, S.C., 1960), pp. 36, 37, 51, 66, 257.

71. *Journal of the House of Representatives of South Carolina, 1782* (Columbia, S.C., 1916), p. 79; R. W. Gibbes, ed., *Documentary History of the American Revolution* (3 vols., New York, 1853–1857), pp. 47–48.

72. Greene to Sumter, April 15, 1781, in *Yearbook of Charleston, 1899*, pp. 89, 90, 93, 102.

73. *A Calm Address to Our American Colonies* (London, 1775).

74. Humanitarian motives are clearly suggested in the "Memorandum on the Right of Englishmen under the 7th Article of the Treaty to withdraw Negroes from the States" (1784). *Shelburne Papers,* 87:389—W. L. Clements Lib.

75. For a recent re-evaluation, see F. B. Tolles, "The American Revolution Considered as a Social Movement," *Amer. Hist. Rev.,* LX (1954), 1–12.

76. Harrell, *op. cit.,* pp. 11, 112.

77. Lefebvre, *op. cit.,* pp. 134, 135.

78. Among the recent studies, see Beatrice G. Rubens, "Pre-Emptive Rights in the Disposition of a Confiscated Estate," *William and Mary Quarterly,* XXII (1965), 435 *et seq.*

79. James Tilghman to Lady Juliana Penn, Chester Town, Md., Aug. 14, 1782. *Shelburne Papers,* 72: 311, William L. Clements Lib.

80. R. E. and B. K. Brown, *Virginia, 1705–1786.* See also R. B. Morris, *Studies in the History of American Law* (New York, 1930), Ch. II; Clarence R. Keim, "The Influence of Primogeniture and Entail in the Development of Virginia" (Ph.D. thesis, Univ. of Chicago, 1926); E. P. Douglass, *Rebels and Democrats* (Chapel Hill, 1955), pp. 300–302.

81. The cost for docking entails after 1767 was £20, along with an additional £2 for every £100 of value of an estate below £500, and £1 for each £100 above that amount. *House Journals,* 1766–1769, p. 113.

82. Hening, *Statutes,* IV, 399–400.

83. The thesis that indebtedness was the key to the actions of the Virginia Patriots between 1774 and 1790 is pressed by I. S. Harrell, *Loyalism in Virginia* (Philadelphia, 1926), and by L. H. Gipson, "Virginia Planter Debts before the American Revolution," *Virginia Mag. of Hist. and Biog.*, LXIX (1961), 259–277. It is questioned by Emory G. Evans, "Planter Indebtedness and the Coming of the American Revolution," *William and Mary Quarterly*, XIX (1962), 511 *et seq.* Thad W. Tate ("The Coming of the Revolution in Virginia," *ibid.*, pp. 323–343) distinguishes between the early years when the debt issue played a minor role and the period beginning with the interruption of the courts in 1774, when it came to the surface.

84. Hening, *Statues at Large of Va.*, IX, 377–388 (1777).

85. W. W. Henry, *Life, Correspondence, and Speeches of Patrick Henry* (3 vols., 1891), II, 187. [Italics mine.]

86. Hening, *Statutes at Large of Va.*, XII, 528, 529 (1787).

87. "Autobiography of John Adams," in L. H. Butterfield, ed., *Diary and Autobiography of John Adams*, III, 326, 327.

88. Reprinted in H. Niles, *Principles and Acts of the Revolution in America* (Baltimore, 1822), p. 402.

III

THE DIPLOMATS
AND THE
MYTHMAKERS

A recent Broadway musical extravaganza reflects the romantic notions many Americans still entertain about the diplomacy of the American Revolution. According to this popular conception, America was so fortunate as to have a shrewd and benevolent sage in France to safeguard and promote her interests, a master diplomat whose democratic garb, severe Quaker black and beaver hat, made him stand out strikingly among the peacocks at Versailles, a man who could exploit flirtation to the advantage of patriotism, who could confound the most devious statesman in direct confrontation, and was able almost single-handedly to persuade La Belle France to come to the rescue of American liberty for purposes largely altruistic.

A roseate hue has always colored our vision of that military marriage of France and America contracted during the War for Independence. For long it was felt that somehow the debt that America owed France remained unpaid. Was not General Pershing reputed to have declared before the tomb of a Revolutionary war hero, "Lafayette, we are here!" Some toiler in historical pastures has unearthed the fact that it was not Pershing but Colonel Charles E. Staunton, a quartermaster officer, who said it, but his words destined for immortality voice the sentiment of a warmhearted and grateful American people.

About their historical relationship Americans and Frenchmen today share mutual disillusionment. To that disillusionment about a shared past much of the credit must go to a charismatic French leader, for *le Général* stands as the best recent exemplar of the truism that in diplomacy "the still small voice of gratitude" is not only small but generally still. Despite the more objective, even acerbic, note that marks exchanges between the First American and the Fifth French Republic, the mythmakers of past generations have done their work so well that the legend of France's disinterested support for the Revolutionary cause has died hard.

One would have expected the sensible views of the diplomats who argued America's cause abroad to prevail, but such expectations fail to discount the depth of anti-British sentiment in America in the generation or two following the American Revolution, and the widespread tendency to regard the enemies of England as the friends of America. Nor should one underestimate the role played by editors in the publication of official documents. This was notably the case in the publication of the diplomatic archives of the American Revolution. Jared Sparks, a member of the intellectual Establishment of his day, president of Harvard College, and confidant of the great and near great, was the first to edit on an extensive scale the diplomatic correspondence of the American Revolution. Sparks set himself up as prosecutor and judge of the actors whose papers he edited and published in garbled versions. Quite rightly did John Quincy Adams, who as a very young man played a small role in the diplomacy of the Revolution abroad, discount the credibility of Sparks' notes by which, he remarked, the record was "impoverished from the hand of the editor." A later and far more objective editor of America's Revolutionary diplomatic documents, Francis Wharton, left out portions of letters he was unable to decipher, often the real meat of the dispatch, and frequently did so without even troubling to inform the reader of the omission. He started out with a pro-French bias that led him to brand as a forgery Barbé-Marbois's notorious dispatch critical of the American claims to the fisheries, although that letter innocently reposes in its proper file in the Quai d'Orsay. In his anxiety to protect the reputation of Franklin, he also felt impelled to exonerate all Franklin's associates from wrongdoing. Thus, he was too gentle with Silas Deane, the American diplomat who finally denounced his own country, and he protested against the recurring innuendoes that Edward Bancroft was a traitor and a spy. Unluckily for Wharton, not too long after his edition was published the Auckland Manuscripts uncovered Bancroft's extraordinary career as a double agent.

Today a substantial portion of the American diplomatic documents have been published, but those of the other belligerents have been largely neglected. Save for fragments, neither the British nor the Spanish documents appear in print, and where, as in the case of France, they have been published, they have been selected and interpreted from a French national viewpoint. The most apt example, the French edition of the dispatches of the Comte de Vergennes, France's magisterial foreign minister, is massive in bulk and conveys an illusion of objective scholarship. In his selective editing and slanted interpretation, Henri Doniol[1] set back the writing of an objective diplomatic history of the American Revolution by several generations. Even where Doniol published a document in full, he accepted the Comte's professions at their face value. As that dean of American diplomatic historians, Samuel Flagg Bemis, has remarked, the Comte put into his dispatches what he wanted his diplomats to say. Like other diplomats he selected, colored, and even invented facts and arguments which he wished to instill. This caution about the Comte's dispatches may fairly be applied to diplomatic dispatches in general for this period. In the first place, they served two levels of government—the responsible officialdom charged with conducting foreign affairs and the secret operatives of the invisible governments. Secondly, while such dispatches can and often do contain extremely frank revelations, they are quite as likely to constitute pieces of special pleading to mask a diplomat's indiscretion or poor judgment.

The obstacles to achieving a sane and thorough appraisal of the diplomacy of the War of the Revolution are no longer so formidable as they were even a generation ago. It may indeed be said that, save for accident or deliberate destruction, the diplomatic records in totality are more fully available to the investigator than at any time since 1783. Prodigies of editorial labors have been expended to assemble the papers of the Founding Fathers and to edit and publish them according to modern standards of historical scholarship. One need only mention the projects now well under way for gathering and publishing the papers of the four American peace commissioners in Paris, Benjamin Franklin, John Adams, John Jay, and Henry Laurens, and the availability in microfilm edition of the massive Papers of the Continental Congress, a rich ore for diplomatic history. New and inexpensive means of photo enlargement have facilitated the task of assembling, organizing, and studying the huge masses of relevant documents that have been gathering dust in distant chancelleries.

Having amassed so huge an inventory, it is perhaps time to take stock. We may well ask whether this fuller documentation has revised our thinking about the diplomacy of the American Revolution, about the nature and course of Franco-American relations and the negotiations to end the war. To what extent must we alter the traditional stereotype?

At the start it might be well to bear in mind that the fuzzy thinking that characterizes the treatment of the Franco-American alliance stems largely from the failure to distinguish between French aid and the formal military pact entered into in 1778. So recently as 1966 a diplomatic historian has asserted, "Without France the Americans were completely helpless."[2] Such indiscriminate confusion, even on the part of reputable scholars, between French aid and France's overt military assistance was not shared by Revolutionary Patriots.

Very early in the conflict, in fact considerably before the Declaration of Independence, American statesmen recognized the importance, even the necessity, of foreign aid if their cause was to meet with success. In July of 1775 Congress, in a Declaration on the Causes and Necessity of Taking Up Arms, a document which we now know Jefferson and John Dickinson composed together, made the point that not only were America's internal resources great but that, *if necessary,* foreign assistance was "undoubtedly attainable."[3] Still Jefferson himself was not yet entirely reconciled to foreign aid. He felt that it might not be obtainable "but in a condition of everlasting revulsion from Great Britain," "a hard condition" indeed, Jefferson added, "to those who still wish for reunion with their parent country."[4]

It is clear that, as the path to reconciliation ended in a thicket, the leading Patriots put their minds to first things first—that is, to foreign aid rather than foreign alliance. No man was more farsighted or outspoken on this score than John Adams. Beyond a commercial alliance with France, Adams was not prepared to go. He suspected the French Court and took a jaundiced view of the way diplomatic operations were conducted at Versailles. An American minister to France might, he ventured in October, 1775, "possibly, if well skill'd in intrigue, his pockets well filled with money and his person robust and elegant enough, get introduced to some of the Misses and Courtesans in keeping of the statesmen of France," but Adams could see no other benefits. Arguing at this time that France was bound to come into the war anyhow, Adams warned that America must avoid alliances which would entangle her in future European wars. This isolationist note was also sounded by Tom Paine, who in *Common Sense* insisted that independence would free the former colonies from being dragged at the heels of England into European wars that were no concern of theirs. Even Benjamin Franklin, often credited, with more generosity than accuracy, with being the architect of the Franco-American alliance, had in the pre-Revolutionary period commented on the disastrous consequences of "our romantick European Continental Connections."[5] When men like Adams and Franklin spoke in these early years about "alliances" they were referring to commercial treaties, not military alliances.[6] In fact, it is quite clear from all the evidence of Franklin's thought and action on the eve of Saratoga that he did not favor pressing France for a military alliance. Not only did he consider it inadvisable to negotiate from weakness, but he still insisted that America could maintain the contest without direct European intervention.[7]

France's aid to America was not impelled by enthusiasm for revolutions against monarchs, but rather was it prompted by a sense of deliberate calculation that such support short of war would enhance her own national interest. France found it opportune to take steps which, while avoiding an open confrontation with her ancient foe, would serve to redress the balance of power against England. That balance, upset by the peace of 1763, might indeed be redressed should England be weakened in a protracted war with her rebellious colonies. The Comte de Vergennes, France's foreign minister, whose caution was legendary, saw to it that the aid should be kept secret and within bounds.[8] So stupendous a secret could not be kept for long, especially since some of those who were privy to it were not noted for their discretion. Not only Silas Deane, who negotiated the original contracts with France, but also the British financier Thomas Walpole, an intimate of Franklin, and the double agent Bancroft, were closely posted on the details of this thinly camouflaged operation. Soon Lord Stormont, Britain's ambassador at Versailles, was to besiege his superiors at home with an unending stream of charges documenting the shipment of arms to America in French armed vessels, legally disguised as privately owned ships. At the start the French provided gunpowder and saltpeter, but as the war intensified and lengthened they shipped heavy guns and mortars, muskets, clothing, blankets, and, most important, substantial sums of hard cash.

Without this French aid, to which the Spaniards initially contributed their mite, the Patriots could not have sustained their military effort, kept their armies in the field, carried out their Fabian tactics, or confronted and conquered the Redcoats and Hessians at Saratoga. It can scarcely be denied, then, that from every point of view *French aid was essential to victory.*

There is another side to the coin, however. Was the French military alliance equally indispensable to the winning of independence? Almost every piece of evidence that is pertinent suggests that it was not. Take, for example, the period of unofficial military assistance prior to the formal alliance when a host of European officers volunteered for the American service. Silas Deane and, later, Benjamin Franklin were overwhelmed in Paris with applications from Frenchmen and other foreigners for high commands in the American army. Most of these officers added very little. Quite a few even contributed to the deterioration of Patriot military morale. Deane conceded that he was "harassed to death" with applications; Robert Morris complained that French officers were flocking over in such numbers that "I don't know what we shall do with them."

Alexander Hamilton, whose pro-French stance during the American Revolution contrasts sharply with his later views, made this measured comment in a letter written from Washington's Morristown headquarters in May, 1777:

> We are already greatly embarrassed with the Frenchmen among us, and from the genius of the people, shall continue to be so. It were to be wished that our agents in France, instead of courting them to come out, were instructed to give no encouragement but where they could not help it; that is, where applications were made to them by persons, countenanced and supported by great men, whom it would be impolitic to disoblige. Be assured, sir, we shall never be able to satisfy them; and they can be of no use to us, at least for some time. Their ignorance of our language, of the disposition of the people, the resources and deficiencies of the country—their own habits and tempers; all these are disqualifications that put it out of their power to be of any real use or service to us. You will consider what I have said entirely as my own sentiments.[9]

Washington, indubitably the best informed of all Americans on the question of army morale and the competence of his officers, complained to Gouverneur Morris in a letter dated White Plains, July 24, 1778, significantly months after the news of the French alliance had reached him. Since the correct text of the Washington original has never been published, it is worth reproducing it in entirety:

24 July 1778, White Plains

DEAR SIR:

Whether you are indebted to me, or I to you, for a Letter, I know not, nor is it a matter of much moment. The design of this is to touch, cursorily, upon a Subject of very great importance to the well-being of these States; much more so than will appear at first view. I mean the appointment of so many to offices of high rank and trust in our service.

The lavish manner in which Rank has hitherto been bestowed on these Gentlemen, will certainly be productive of one, or the other of these two evils, either, to make it despicable in the eyes of Europe, or, become a mean of pouring them in upon you like a torrent, and adding to your present burthen—but it is neither the expence nor trouble of them I most dread—there is an evil more extensive in its nature, and fatal in its consequences to be apprehended, and that is, the driving all your own officers out of the Service, and throwing not only your Arms, but your Military Councils, entirely in the hands of Foreigners.

The Officers, my dear Sir, on whom you must depend for defence of this cause, and who from length of Service —their connexions—property—and (in behalf of many) I may add, military merit, will not submit much, if any longer, to the unnatural promotion of men over them, who have nothing more than a little plausibility—unbounded pride and ambition—and a perseverance in application, which is not to be resisted but by uncommon firmness, to support their pretensions—Men, who in the first instance tell you, that they wish for nothing more than the honour of serving in so glorious a cause, as Volunteers—The next day sollicit Rank without pay—the day following want money advanced them—and in the course of a Week want further promotion, and are not satisfied with any thing you can do for them.

When I speak of Officers not submitting to these appointments, let me be understood to mean, that they have no more doubt of their right to resign (when they think themselves aggrieved), than they have of a power in Congress to appoint—both being granted then, the expedience, & the policy of the measure remain to be considered; & whether, it is consistent with justice, or prudence, to promote these military fortune hunters at the hazard of your Army—especially as I think they may be denominated into three classes—to wit mere adventurers without recommendation or recommended by persons who do not know how else to dispose of, or provide for them—Men of great ambition, who would sacrifice every thing to promote their own personal glory—or, mere spies, who are sent here to obtain a thorough knowledge of our situation, circumstances etc.; in the executing of which, I am persuaded, some of them are faithful emissaries, as I do not believe a single matter escapes unnoticed, or unadvised, at a foreign Court.

I could say a great deal on this subject, but will add no more at present. I am led to give you this trouble at this time, by a *very handsome* certificate shewed me yesterday in favor of M. Neville, written (I believe) by himself; and subscribed by General Parsons, designed, as I am informed, for a foundation of the superstructure of a Brigadiership.

Baron Steuben I now find is also wanting to quit his Inspectorship for a command in the line, this will also be productive of much discontent to the Brigadiers. In a word, altho I think the Baron an excellent Officer, I do most devoutly wish that we had not a single Foreigner among us, except the Marquis de la Fayette, who acts upon very different principles than those which govern the rest. Adieu. I am most sincerely yours,

GEORGE WASHINGTON

P.S. This Letter, as you will perceive, is written with the

freedom of a friend do not therefore make me enemys by publishing what is intended for your own information & that of particular friends.[10]

Whether the French were induced to align themselves openly on America's side out of conviction, following news of the victory at Saratoga, that the Americans could win, or whether, as a recent diplomatic historian has argued, the French and Spaniards, to judge from the formidable naval power they had amassed in the West Indies by the fall of '77, had planned an overt intervention even before news reached Europe of Burgoyne's surrender[11] seems beside the point. What triggered the French alliance was the desperate fear that gripped the French Ministry that the British were about to come to terms with America. It is not by coincidence that the alliance came on the eve of Parliament's authorization of what proved to be the ill-fated Carlisle Peace Mission to America, a mission that was prepared to offer everything to America that would have prevented conflict in 1775, but too little now and too late.

It has been tediously repeated time on end that without the assistance of French naval and military forces in the Chesapeake area the Patriots could not have prevailed at Yorktown. How can one deny one of the most venerated of all historical clichés? The fortuitous presence of de Grasse's fleet, sealing off rescue or reinforcements for the hard-pressed Cornwallis, and the sizable and effective French land force under Rochambeau were essential factors in Washington's victory.

One might well speculate, though, whether the war might have been ended on terms favorable to the Patriots long before Yorktown had it not been for the French alliance. In estimating the effectiveness of French military intervention one must bear in mind that it took the French almost three and a half years to mount an offensive land and sea force that could work in cooperation with the Americans. All previous efforts were fiascoes. 'The first fleet under d'Estaing, which entered Delaware Bay in July of 1778 to find that the British had already departed, comprised ships too large to get past the bar at Sandy Hook. Instead of bottling up the inferior British fleet in New York Harbor, d'Estaing moved his ships to Rhode Island, only to infuriate the Patriot General Sullivan by refusing to cooperate in capturing the British garrison at Newport. Moved on to Boston, d'Estaing's men outraged the inhabitants, with whom they had armed clashes. In effect, d'Estaing's inept performance induced men as different in personality but as ardent in their patriotism as Jefferson and Lee to reflect on the possibility of an advantageous peace with Britain.[12] But that was not to be the last of d'Estaing. In the early fall of '79 he besieged British-held Savannah, where he was joined by General Lincoln. Although the Franco-American amphibious force outnumbered the British defenders by almost two to one, the former were repulsed with casualties more than five times those of the Redcoats.

Indeed, the year 1779 was a disastrous one for the French on all fronts. That year Spain secretly joined the war as a cobelligerent of France but not as an ally of the insurgent Americans. The two Continental allies, without confiding in the Americans, embarked upon a daring combined operation to invade England, an operation comparable in magnitude to the great armada of two centuries earlier. Yet the Franco-Spanish allies let a golden opportunity slip through their fingers. The dismal motions of the combined fleets in Channel waters made clear to the French just what they might expect from the Spanish pact. In turn, the Spaniards became increasingly pessimistic in their estimates of France's ability to prosecute the war. With the year 1779 ending in a deadly stalemate on both the military and diplomatic fronts, peace held more appeal to the Bourbon partners than it had back in the spring. Spain's principal minister, the Conde de Floridablanca, now bent his mind to ways of quitting the war with both honor and profit, and in France disillusionment and division encouraged the appeasers. In short, a strong case could be made to support the argument that, barring Yorktown, an event which caught France and Spain completely by surprise, the Franco-Spanish belligerents might have brought pressure on America to accept a peace short of full independence, and that such pressure might well have proved irresistible.

Apart from the hapless Dutch, who entered the war very late and hardly of their own volition, the addition of France and Spain as belligerents complicated and tangled the war aims of the coalition arrayed against Great Britain. It is hardly news at this late date that the war aims of Spain and France differed from those of America and even conflicted at various points. Spain's insistence on continuing the war until Gibraltar was regained, a point to which France agreed, threatened to lengthen the conflict for objectives to which the Americans had not committed themselves in their treaty of alliance with France. Regardless of the justice of the rival claims, Spain opposed America's westward ambitions as threatening her own colonial empire and France sedulously and systematically discouraged America from mounting a second invasion of Canada, which she did not mean to see added as a Fourteenth State. Nor was France at all happy about America's claim to fishing rights off the Grand Bank which New Englanders had so profitably enjoyed as British colonists but had seemingly forfeited as rebels.[13]

Finally, regardless of the estimate one places on French military intervention down to the summer of 1781, there is no question but that France's overt entry into the war prevented the overthrow of the North Ministry in 1778 and delayed that turnover until after Yorktown. It was a body blow to the appeasers among the Whigs, who, of

course, were traditionally anti-French, and thus succeeded in uniting a divided England against an ancient
foe as it had not previously been united in its war against
the Americans. It made a detested war respectable and
patriotic, and for a brief time at least enormously
strengthened the hands of both the North Ministry and
the King. When one of the British peace commissioners
was informed by a rebel leader that France was sure to
join the war, he replied: "We must consider you then as
Frenchmen; the contest has changed; and so we must
prosecute the war."[14]

If, then, the French military alliance was at least as
much a liability as it was an asset to the ultimate American military victory, how must we evaluate the impact of
the alliance on the chief ends of American diplomacy? In
answering that question we are confronted with one of
the most sedulously cultivated myths of the American
Revolution. Concocted and perpetuated by partisan
diplomatic historians and biographers, the myth piously
affirms that France was faithful to her alliance of 1778
with the United States, and that the American commissioners demonstrated an unwarranted distrust of the
Comte de Vergennes when, in a moment of disloyalty,
they negotiated a separate Preliminary Peace with
England.

Numerous facets of this controversy have been dealt
with at considerable length in *The Peacemakers*,[15] and no
capsule summary can do justice either to the participants
in the diplomacy of those years or to the issues with
which they came to grips. Without doing violence to
essential detail, one can, however, establish a few basic
points briefly. First, it should be pointed out that within a
year after she had made her alliance with the United
States, France broke the spirit if not the letter of her two
treaties with America. The secret pact of Aranjuez she
entered into with Spain violated France's treaty of com-

merce with the United States in the stipulation therein made to share the fishery *only* with Spain provided she could drive the British from Newfoundland. The French commitment to continue the war until Gibraltar should be taken amounted to a unilateral change in the terms of the treaty between France and America.

The American commissioners should have trusted Vergennes. From Jared Sparks to Orville Murphy critics have so contended, implying that the commissioners were guilty of disloyalty to France by having signed the Preliminaries separately and negotiated them secretly. Their arguments, it must be answered, seem fallacious on several scores. In the first place, the critics of the commissioners assume that the government of France had but a single voice on foreign policy, and that the voice of the Comte de Vergennes. It would be equally as unrealistic to assume that the foreign policy of Secretary of State Jefferson mirrored the position of President Washington or that the foreign policy of Charles James Fox reflected fully the Rockingham-Shelburne Ministry. Thanks to Julian Boyd, we now know how Alexander Hamilton, as self-constituted prime minister in Washington's administration, tried to push his own foreign policy, and passed on to the British agent Beckwith as administrative views ideas which were very personal to him. He did not neglect to do the same at the time of Jay's Treaty, as we have long known. Likewise it should be noted that the French Ministry was riddled by faction, court politics, and intrigue, and that others in that Ministry failed to see eye to eye with Vergennes, specifically as regards the goal of American independence. Feeling strongly that Vergennes's policies would lead to ruin, they took it upon themselves to initiate their own negotiations with the enemy, negotiations which, if consummated, would have been damaging if not fatal to American independence.

A real push toward peace got under way during the

summer of 1780 from inside the French Court but without the knowledge of its foreign minister. The fall of Charleston to the British shook French confidence in America's will to win; the plan to redeem paper at a 40-to-1 ratio evoked shrieks of anguish from Parisian bankers, war contractors, and speculators, and caused still another contretemps between John Adams and Vergennes. Joseph II had gone off to Mogilev to talk with Catherine for reasons that were not clear to Vergennes, but which boded ill for France's aspirations as the arbiter of Europe. At San Ildefonso Floridablanca was toying with the British emissary, Richard Cumberland, and implanting deep suspicions among French diplomats that Spain was ready to quit the war.

Troubles were even closer to home. At Versailles Jacques Necker, director general of the Treasury and of finances, submitted the Treasury accounts to a fresh audit. During the late summer of 1780 he informed Comte Maurepas, the ailing octogenarian first minister, that he had discovered a serious discrepancy in those accounts. "A blow of a bomb," he called it, "as unexpected as it is unbelievable." Estimated taxes would not make up this deficiency, and another huge war loan would sit perilously atop the vast debt already accumulated, the Swiss banker warned. The only sensible course, Necker urged, was to come to terms with the enemy.

Maurepas was now ready to desert the war, and the King himself was perilously poised. Vergennes managed to persuade Louis XVI to continue the war effort, and even wrung from Maurepas his reluctant consent to the fateful third campaign in America, the one that would prove decisive. At the same time France's foreign minister now turned to the idea of outside mediation, as a more suitable alternative to self-abasement.

What Vergennes does not seem to have realized was that earlier that summer, doubtless under pressure from

Necker, Comte Maurepas had sent out a peace feeler to Lord North, using as an intermediary a dissolute, loose-tongued Englishman named Nathaniel Parker Forth, who had served in the past as an agent of the British government in France. Since the North Ministry had another iron in the fire, the Cumberland-Floridablanca negotiations at San Ildefonso, which from a distance still held some promise, it was disinclined to become too heavily involved with the French at this time, and clearly would not be rushed. Judging from papers later turned over to Lord Shelburne, it appears that Maurepas on this occasion, and perhaps as early as the late fall of 1779, was prepared to accept an armistice, which would allow the British to keep possession of what they then held in America, and a restitution of any conquests made by France, Spain, or Great Britain since the treaty of Fontainebleau of 1762.

This was not the last we are to hear of the fatal truce proposal. In the early fall of 1780 Thomas Walpole, a London banker and a close associate of Necker, proposed to Maurepas's intimate friend, the Abbé Véri, that a truce would resolve the difficulty posed by American independence, and on the basis of such encouragement as Véri could offer him after talking to Maurepas, Walpole dispatched a letter to North with a truce proposal. George III turned it down not only because he found Walpole politically unpalatable but also because he would not enter into negotiations with France so long as American independence was "an article of their propositions."

Meantime in France the crisis was drawing nearer. Maurepas was laid low by illness; Sartine and Montbarrey, the ministers of marine and war, were dropped as a result of Necker's agitation. Now Necker's star was in the ascendant, and it seemed doubtful that Vergennes could hold on much longer. While he had not yet managed to supplant Vergennes, Necker assumed some of the foreign minister's functions and put out peace feelers on his own, using as intermediary his former tutor, Paul-Henri Mallet, a Swiss professor and historian. By chance Mallet also had been a tutor and companion to Viscount Mountstuart, the British ambassador to Turin, who possessed some of the theatricality that his father, Lord Bute, had once abundantly demonstrated. Mountstuart, taking a summer vacation in Geneva, conferred with Mallet, the latter having only just returned from a long stay in Paris, where he had talked freely with his former pupil, M. Necker. The essence of Necker's conversation was that France needed peace desperately, that the only thing that was holding up that peace for a single minute was the American rebellion. A notorious Anglophile, Necker was quoted by Mallet as expressing the fervent hope "in God the English would be able to maintain their ground a little better this campaign." In a search for a formula Mallet proposed to Necker that "some one province," say New England, be declared independent, "and the others obliged to return to their former allegiance." Necker's response was favorable, but he talked in general terms, avoiding specific details.

Mallet carried on a number of talks with Mountstuart along these lines and agreed to go to Paris to ascertain whether the French Ministry was serious about terms of peace. From Geneva the British ambassador rushed by a personal servant a report of these conversations to Hillsborough, England's obtuse secretary of state. Even before he had heard from home, Mountstuart was the recipient of a series of letters sent by Mallet concerning his proposed Paris mission. Mountstuart then wrote again to Hillsborough proposing to join Mallet in Paris, using some pretext, such as poor health, to necessitate his trip.

The official answer finally arrived. On November 21st Hillsborough wrote Mountstuart that he had laid his communications before the King, who, in accordance with his rigid formula, refused to discuss terms with France so long as she continued to aid and abet the rebellion in America. In a rather stinging rebuke Hillsborough made the point that such unavowed and private talks were unauthorized and that it would be improper for the British ambassador to go to Paris.

How heavily Necker counted upon the Mallet-Mountstuart conversations we perhaps will never know, but as winter was approaching and the British envoy from Turin failed to appear in Paris, Necker became increasingly restive. Peace, no matter of what kind, was essential if war prospects did not improve, Necker was quoted by Austria's ambassador as having remarked. He was prepared to go behind Vergennes's back and effect a peace without satisfying even the minimum goals of France's two allies and without regard to Louis XVI's own honored commitments.

On December 1st Necker, in the full assurance of his growing power, dispatched a secret message to Lord North, "for you alone, my Lord," in which he proposed a truce "more or less long," during which the belligerent parties in America could hold "in a sovereign manner" the territory they now possessed there. North passed the letter on to George III, who, with his habitual promptness, gave the customary answer—a truce is another form of independence, and until France gave up that objective peace was out of the question. The next day North sent off to Necker, "in a feigned Italian hand" and under conditions of secrecy, a note incorporating the substance of the King's response and repulsing the Director-General's personal peace move.

One might well speculate on what the subsequent course of world history might have been had George III encouraged Necker's desperate intervention to halt the war. The Director-General's idea of a truce of varying duration was only an echo of an idea that Floridablanca had thrown out as far back as April, 1779, when the

Spanish minister proposed the *uti possidetis* for the
United States, and that proposition was to be warmed
over and served up from time to time by Russian and
Austrian mediators. That a settlement in the early winter
of 1780–81 on the basis of territories then effectively
controlled by each side would have chopped up the Thirteen United States into little pieces and prevented the
establishment of a viable nation did not appear to perturb
Necker. Having first thought quite seriously about a tiny
northeastern federation of quasi-independent states, he
was now prepared to settle for a nation comprising New
England, the Middle States without the port of New York,
and a fractured and blighted Southland lacking all access
to the sea.

Time, however, was running out for Necker. With the
compte rendu he shot his bolt, and his enemies marshaled
their forces to smash the power-hungry Director-General
and the formidable peace party he headed. Though
master of the Ministry following Necker's forced resignation on May 19, 1781, Vergennes was visibly shaken by
the struggle. The combined dosage of appeasement administered through the separate efforts of Floridablanca
and Necker now predisposed him to consider a truce on
terms not too far removed from his adversaries'. The only
difference was that the Foreign Minister would not accept
so unpalatable a prescription from any physician other
than outside mediators. Vergennes's approach to a truce,
as we shall see, had a subtle difference from Necker's, to
be sure, but the consequences could have been equally
ruinous to the young republic across the Atlantic.

Mountstuart merely licked his wounds and bided his
time for another foray into the diplomatic jungle, and in
the spring of 1782, with Charles James Fox's encouragement, he sought to reopen negotiations with the French
through Mallet, only to learn how low Necker's stock had
fallen. Whether inadvertently or not, the new British

administration found a role for Mountstuart to play in the peacemaking, and at a strategic moment. Granted leave to return home, he reached Paris on December 18, 1782, a little over a fortnight after the Americans signed the preliminary peace but before France and Spain had completed their own preliminaries. On December 22nd he dined with Richard Oswald, Britain's negotiator with the Americans. That same evening John Jay made a social call upon the British peace commissioner. Oswald, as Jay recorded in his diary, told him that Lord Mountstuart, who "execrated the American War," had brought along his letterbooks, "which he did not chuse to leave with his chargé d'affaires." Oswald was permitted to read the correspondence with Hillsborough, beginning in September, 1780, reporting the overtures made by Necker through Mallet as intermediary, reputedly "about putting an end to the war by dividing America between Britain and France, the latter to have the eastern part." To hammer the point home, Mountstuart read Oswald from his letterbook of French letters the Mallet correspondence, revealing, as Jay summarized it, Necker's concern that the expenses of the war would disarray his financing and perhaps bring about his disgrace. Jay was also informed "that the overtures about America were conducted with a variety of precautions for secrecy and with a stipulation or condition that both parties, in case they did not agree, should be at liberty to deny all that passed." Mountstuart conceded that Hillsborough had told him that "the subject was out of his line." Of course, the Mallet correspondence never explicitly proposed such a division between France and England, although the formula for a settlement was left purposely vague, and much else might have been suggested in the Mallet-Mountstuart talks that was never recorded.

By coincidence the identical terms were allegedly offered by Vergennes to a British visitor, on the word of

Sir William Pulteney, who several years before had secretly offered Benjamin Franklin what the British then considered liberal peace terms. Oswald had previously relayed to Jay and Adams Pulteney's completely undocumented assertion that Vergennes had offered to end the war by dividing America with Britain, "and in case the latter agreed to the partition, that the force of France and Britain should be used to reduce it to the obedience of the respective sovereigns." Pulteney's story was somebody's baseless concoction—"Whispers which should not be credited to us," Adams put it—but the Turin letterbooks of Mountstuart provided Oswald with just enough corroboration to hammer home the point that America's ally was prepared to sell her out at any time. Jay passed the "extraordinary story" on to Adams. Whether or not Jay was taken in, his liveliest suspicions had already been aroused, not only by his long exposure to double-dealing in Spain but more recently by the secret peace mission that Vergennes' undersecretary Rayneval undertook to England in the fall of '82.

Years later Edmond Genêt took it upon himself to deny that the Necker-Mallet-Mountstuart negotiations had ever taken place. He managed to do this by mistaking the time of the negotiations for 1782, when Necker was out of office, instead of 1780, when the banker was at the height of his power, and by blandly asserting that Necker had never interfered in the concerns of the department of foreign affairs. His error was compounded, for at the date in question Genêt's father, Edmé Jacques Genêt, was *premier commis* of the Bureau of Interpretation, and Genêt was a chargé in Vienna. Edmé held the post until September, 1781, when on his death his precocious son, then a minor functionary, succeeded him. By that date Necker was no longer in office but he had seen to it that his negotiations looking toward a peace were carefully concealed from Vergennes and his subordinates. We know

now what really happened despite the weak disclaimer of a petty functionary, long removed in time and place from the feverish events he was describing.

From our vantage point it seems transparently clear that a truce on the basis of the ground possessed would almost any time before Yorktown, and even possibly thereafter, have been admitting the wolf into the sheep-fold and have imperiled the very independence for which the Thirteen States were battling. Yet by February, 1781, as Samuel Flagg Bemis has made clear, the Comte de Vergennes was prepared to be persuaded by the mediating powers, Russia and Austria, of the virtues of ending the war on the basis of such a formula, only excepting New York, which the British would have to evacuate. American attendance at a peace congress determined by such a formula would have resolved a dilemma posed by the new Revolutionary nation, even though the independence of the United States might have been sacrificed as a result thereof.

The credit for concocting this subtle evasion of the pledge not to end the war until American independence was obtained must be shared by diplomats of several nations. It was the brain child of several chancelleries. First, the initial formula was the invention of Count Panin, Russia's chancellor. In the late summer of 1780 he proposed to the Comte de Vérac, France's ambassador at St. Petersburg, that during the proposed armistice the King of France could require *each* of the Thirteen States to declare its intention; thereafter he would only be obliged to maintain the independence of those states who wished to keep it. If some, for example, the two Carolinas, preferred the path of submission, then the "point of honor" of France would be satisfied, as the engagement toward them would be annulled. Vergennes immediately perceived how this formula would resolve the great issue of American independence by cutting what the diplomats loved to call "the Gordian knot of the present war." Vergennes, who privately believed that a separate polling, colony by colony as Panin advised, would have resulted in a vote for partition, now came out for an immediate armistice of at least four or five years and separate consultations with each of the states regarding their wish to maintain their independence. As of that date, the Comte was prepared to turn back to the British the whole of the Lower South, which was what Panin's shrewd formula would have meant.

Panin's second proposal was that *each* of the "united colonies of America" send delegates to a European peace Congress, delegates who would be accountable to their respective assemblies and not to Congress. In fact, that federal body was to remain suspended until each province had ruled on its fate.

At this point the British, with their skill at diplomatic maneuver, fearful that Panin was biased against them, brought Austria in as a comediator, and in effect the notion of a peace congress was transferred to Vienna, with the Austrian Chancellor, Prince von Kaunitz, rather than Panin, holding the center of the stage. Kaunitz pounced upon the Panin plan and proposed that each state send a deputy to the Congress to treat separately of its affairs with England. Not being privy to the Panin-Vérac-Vergennes correspondence, the French ambassador to Vienna, Baron de Breteuil, insisted that the American negotiations be confined to "as few hands as possible." To his amazement, he was immediately repudiated. Vergennes instructed him to accept Kaunitz's proposal, and specifically endorsed the Panin-Kaunitz plan of having the separate state legislatures choose their own peace deputies. Perhaps a little bewildered by his new instructions, Breteuil was unable to obtain from Kaunitz a clarification of the notion of thirteen American deputies instead of a solitary delegate before the mediators adopted a series of preliminary points to serve as a basis of negotiations. These points included a one-year armistice during which everything should remain *in statu quo.*

Although Great Britain was teetering on the brink of one of the great military defeats of her history, her Ministry was not prepared to make the concessions that these preliminary bases required of her. As Graf von Belgiojoso, Austria's envoy to London, reported, the British still refused to negotiate with the rebels. They would consider nothing less than their submission, and had no intention of treating with the Americans at Vienna. Indeed, a strange complacency gripped the British Ministry. Only a few days before news reached London of the surrender of Cornwallis, Lord Stormont, Britain's secretary of state, told Russian Ambassador Simolin that England would not recognize the independence of America until the French took the Tower of London, and that she would exchange Gibraltar only for Madrid. France reacted to the turn in the military tide by viewing with a jaundiced eye the one-year armistice and the provision for the *status quo,* both of which Undersecretary Gérard de Rayneval pointed out might well be objected to by the Americans. Vergennes now told Vérac that France had no right to stipulate for the United States, and if she did she would run the risk of being disavowed.

Behind Vergennes's sudden caution about America lay an important interview with John Adams. The New Englander warned Vergennes that any truce would be productive of "another long and bloody war at the termination of it" and a short truce would be especially dangerous. Vergennes was affrighted at the thought of the incorrigible New Englander's scurrying off to Vienna to run the show his own way. Any day now the Comte was expecting word that Adams had been supplanted by Congress or that a plural peace mission in which Adams had but one voice would assume his duties. Somehow Adams had gotten wind of the Panin-Kaunitz scheme of separate consultations with each of the Thirteen States and in his most didactic vein he proceeded to lecture Vergennes on the Articles of Confederation and to point out that the power to negotiate with foreign nations was expressly delegated therein to Congress. Vergennes dared not disregard Adams' stern warning. In the winter of '81 the French foreign minister had seriously considered a partition of America. In the late spring he had revitalized the notion of negotiating a settlement with the deputies from each of the Thirteen States. After Adams' summer interlude in Paris, Vergennes was less inclined to speak for America, as regards both the terms of an armistice and the question of representation at the proposed Congress. Truly, Mr. Adams had put a spoke in the wheel, and the mediation, to America's gain, soon ground to a halt. So much, then, for the notion that America should trust Vergennes.

Another myth of the peacemaking sedulously cultivated by diplomatic historians writing within the old French-alliance frame of reference is the charge that John Jay, the American peace commissioner who joined Franklin in Paris in the late spring of 1782, was of an inordinately suspicious nature and allowed his overstrained views of national dignity to jeopardize the peace negotiations up to then in the capable hands of Benjamin Franklin. The hackneyed charges against Mr. Jay include the count that the New Yorker, by his insistence on making the recognition of the United States a precondition to entering upon negotiations, held up the Preliminaries, with the result that the United States obtained less in November of 1782 than it could have won in August or September. In *The Peacemakers,* Lord Shelburne has been closely pursued in the zigzag course he followed during these months. Therein it has been shown that not only was the Earl's position equivocal, even vis-à-vis his own intimate associates, but that there was a point beyond which he could not go if (1) he wished to retain the support of the King and (2) he expected to maintain his slim and rapidly diminishing hold upon Parliament.

What are at issue are not the bases of Jay's suspicions of the British government, suspicions incontrovertibly corroborated by the evidence now available, but rather whether there was any substance to Jay's fears about the course France was pursuing. The New Yorker has been castigated for acting upon his conviction that the French were about to double-cross their American ally either by making a separate deal with England apart from the Thirteen States or by delaying an American settlement until the Spaniards could recapture Gibraltar, a delusive hope as it turned out. Here the timetable of negotiations takes on special significance. On August 10, 1782, Franklin and Jay journeyed to Versailles, and were told by the Comte de Vergennes that there was no point in America's insisting upon explicit recognition in advance, that an exchange of commissions would serve the purpose of formal recognition. Franklin, who for months had opposed entering upon negotiations with the British without securing such explicit recognition in advance, now meekly conceded that it "would do." Contrariwise, Jay let Vergennes know that the formula did not satisfy him and that he deemed it best to proceed cautiously. To Lafayette Vergennes dictated a formula providing for the complete renunciation of sovereignty by the first article of the treaty. At that same meeting Rayneval frankly told the Americans that, so far as the West was concerned, they claimed more than they had a right to.

On their way home Jay turned to Franklin and denounced France for wanting America to remain under her direction "until not only their and our objects are attained" but also until Spain should be gratified in her demand to exclude everybody from the Gulf and the Mississippi. The secret documents now available to historians prove that Jay was correct in his appraisal of the situation, that since the beginning of July Floridablanca had been pressing Vergennes to defer recognition of the insurgents until a general peace. Otherwise the Americans, once content, he argued, might drop out of the war before Gibraltar was secured.

Thus, more than a quibble was involved. Shelburne and the Cabinet for bargaining reasons would not concede independence in advance; Vergennes was concerned lest the Americans drop out of the war should they attain their objective. So shrewd an observer of the international scene as the Comte Mercy d'Argenteau, Austria's ambassador to Versailles, felt that the English Cabinet, by raising the legal issue of the King's power to concede independence, were giving themselves a loophole to cut off negotiations. Jay wanted this hole plugged before going ahead.

So far as France was concerned, the formula proposed by Vergennes to the American was devised for the very purpose of having Great Britain put off recognizing the Americans until the final peace. The Foreign Minister of France made that clear himself. Not long after his August 10th conference with Jay and Franklin he remarked to the British envoy, Alleyne Fitzherbert, that he had advised the Americans to defer their insistence on actual recognition by Great Britain until the final peace rather than seek it as a preliminary to negotiating. Vergennes's amazing indiscretion revealed the split between the allies on a burning issue and confirmed the suspicions of the British Foreign Secretary Lord Grantham that "the granting Independency to America as a previous measure is a point which the French have no means at heart, and perhaps are entirely averse from." The British, as one might expect, made sure that Jay was told how Vergennes had crossed him behind his back. Small wonder that John Jay concluded the policy of the Comte de Vergennes was "to keep America in leading strings." Indeed, massive evidence reposing in the Archives of the Quai d'Orsay provides solid and overwhelming refutation of the contention of the French Foreign Office that the opinions on the fisheries or the West attributed to subordinates were purely personal to them and did not reflect the official policy of the French Court.

On August 29th the British Cabinet secretly decided to agree to Franklin's terms, which provided a more generous northern boundary than the United States finally was forced to accept. That the decision could have served as the basis for the round of preliminary talks still ahead is highly dubious, however. It is hardly conceivable that a Cabinet decision that ignored the issue of compensating the Tories and guaranteeing debts due the British creditors would have been ratified by Parliament even if the British Ministry had committed itself to the Americans on the basis of the August 29th understanding. The fact is that the Ministry did no such thing. It kept the decision secret and continued to withhold information from John Jay about its intentions. Why should the British Ministry have followed so devious a course? The explanation seems ready at hand. The British government was well aware of Vergennes' anxiety that the concession on independence be deferred until the treaty itself. Furthermore, they were also aware, apparently through information provided by the turncoat Edward Bancroft, that John Jay was prepared to hold the Comte de Vergennes responsible for any delays on the part of London.

Three circumstances now impelled John Jay to take the initiative. Around this time the British placed in Jay's hand an intercepted letter from the French Secretary of Legation in America in which the indiscreet Barbé-Marbois back in March of 1782 had expressed his hostility to the claims of America to a share in the Newfoundland fisheries and cautioned his government against New England's current outcry, "No peace without the fisheries." Almost coincidentally with the revelations contained in the fisheries' letter, Gérard de Rayneval, French Undersecretary of Foreign Affairs, had turned over to Jay a memorandum supporting in substance Spain's claims to a substantial share of the territory west of the Appalachians claimed by America for her own. This memorandum, whose general lines had been forecast in numerous conversations between Jay and Rayneval, convinced the American that the French Foreign Ministry was hardly neutral in the dispute raging behind the scenes between Spain and America over the western boundaries.

What triggered Jay's extraordinary response, however, was the revelation that on September 7th Rayneval had taken off for England incognito. Like so many other well-guarded diplomatic secrets, Rayneval's absence was bruited about almost at once and caused a buzz of speculation. Vergennes, while notifying the Spaniards of the mission, did not trouble to inform the Americans. To Jay the gossip about the Undersecretary's pseudo-secret mission sounded an alarm bell in the night. Later critics of John Jay who were not privy to the negotiations have relied heavily on Rayneval's formal instructions which contained nothing about America's claims, but Rayneval's own report of his conversations belies the assertions that he did not advert to America. First of all, Rayneval told Shelburne that the "King would never support an unjust demand" as regards America's claims to the fisheries. A week earlier Shelburne's own Cabinet had decided to concede the Americans a share in the fisheries. Now Rayneval told Shelburne: "We do not want the Americans to share in the fisheries." This was enough to stiffen British counterdemands on that score. As regards the boundaries, Rayneval in his first visit assured Shelburne that it was the King's intention to "contain the Americans within the bounds of justice and reason." He even talked about the 1754 negotiations relative to the Ohio, a point which he had also made in the memoir he had left in Jay's hands before his hurried departure for London. The application of the rule of 1754, as Rayneval interpreted it, would have barred America from the Old Northwest.

Emboldened by the support of the French Court implied in Rayneval's remarks, as well as by the heartening news to come of the successful defense of Gibraltar, Shelburne was to renege the Cabinet offer of August 29th and to put up one more desperate stand along the Ohio. According to Shelburne's own account, Rayneval gave him to understand that, once independence was granted, the French "were disposed to assist us as to the Boundaries."

Quick to perceive the peril to American interests at the peacemaking should France and England arrive at a secret understanding, Jay took the most audacious step of his career. He dispatched a pro-American intermediary, Benjamin Vaughan, a quasi agent of Shelburne's, to England on a mission so secret that neither Vergennes nor Franklin was apprised of it. Vaughan was given a compromise proposal for recognition, and on his arrival in England the Cabinet voted to concede Jay's point and to issue a new commission to Richard Oswald empowering him to treat and conclude "with any Commission or person vested with equal power by and on the part of the Thirteen United States of America." At long last the rebellious states had been recognized by the mother country, and the peacemaking could now proceed to its successful conclusion.

The diplomacy of the American Revolution suggests all sorts of tantalizing analogies to the recent past and the troubled present. One may see striking parallels between the negotiations of 1782–1783 involving the Great Powers and the American colonists and the long and protracted parleys some years back between the French government and the Algerian rebels. The American Commissioners, it must be remembered, sought not only independence but territorial integrity and elbow room. One might compare their insistence upon the inclusion of the trans-Appalachian West with the demands pressed by the Algerian nationalists to the French Sahara. America's case was perhaps no stronger, either juridically or morally, for it rested its claims to the West upon vague charter provisions conferred by the English Crown which it had repudiated, and these claims, like the Algerian, were not bolstered by effective military occupation. It must be borne in mind that the bulk of the territory George Rogers Clark had conquered in the Northwest had largely slipped from America's grip by the close of the war. All the Great Powers opposed America's obtaining the West, and indubitably the claims of both Spain and England to that region were strong ones. But after a partition of the American continent, which everybody but America wanted, the new republic would not have been left with a durable fragment. Similarly, the partition of Algeria according to the myriad plans that were put forth would not have assured the FLN a viable state, nor would the secession of Katanga or Oriente province have allowed the Congo the wherewithal to survive and prosper.

The Algerian negotiations suggest a still further analogy to the American Revolutionary settlement. In both sets of negotiations the Loyalists posed a thorny problem. The latter comprised the American Tories, the former the large European community in Algeria. In both cases the rights and grievances of this substantial segment of the population loyal to the mother country posed formidable obstacles to concluding any agreement. Neither settlement effectively protected the Loyalists in fact and both were followed by mass Loyalist emigrations.

Even more tantalizing is the analogy between King

George III's obstinate course in refusing to recognize the insurgent Americans who held part but not all of the Thirteen States and the refusal of the United States to deal directly with the Viet Cong who held part if not all of Vietnam. Obviously there are limits to which the latter analogy can be pressed, as the United States was never a colonial power in Indo-China. Unlike the British in 1776, the Americans in Vietnam are ostensibly fighting for the principle of self-determination by a former colonial people beset by internal subversion and foreign aggression. Regrettably, there has been a corroding confusion about the objectives of America's intervention, objectives which critics put under the rubric of "neo-colonialism." But then "neo-colonialism" as it is used in the Asiatic world is a pejorative word, and many Asiatics, perhaps unfairly, regard America as assuming the mantle of France in Southeast Asia. Finally, the point might be made that during the American Revolution, though Congress first demanded that, as a precondition to entering upon negotiations, the British army leave the Thirteen Colonies, our peacemakers did not lay down such preconditions. They were too realistic to insist on conditions that would be insupportable to the pride of a Great Power or that they were in fact unable to effectuate.

In his Godkin Lectures the late Adlai Stevenson pointed out that "we shall have to learn" that "we cannot deal with questions of foreign policy in terms of moral absolutes." Stevenson went on to observe: "Compromise is not immoral or treasonable. It is the objective of negotiation and negotiation is the means of resolving conflict peacefully. But when we negotiate we have to have something to negotiate with as well as for. If rigidity and absolutist attitudes relieve our representatives of anything to negotiate with, then there is nothing they can negotiate for."

To be sure, the hand of the Americans in Paris was strengthened by the results of Yorktown, after which they could negotiate from victory, because an obdurate enemy will enter into negotiations only when it recognizes that it can no longer win. What was especially distinctive about our American diplomats in Paris in 1782–1783, aside from their effectiveness, was their style. With skill and audacity they wielded the weapons of Revolutionary diplomacy, confident in the strength and promise of the new nation they represented. This confidence in America's future was by no means shared by European statesmen. Rather, they expected America to suffer the lethargy of other republics, a lethargy compounded by sectional rivalries. Almost gleefully did they anticipate division and secession, hopefully expecting some day that the Great Powers would come in and pick up the pieces.

In that great confrontation of the Old Order and the New which the negotiations between the diplomats of the Great Powers and the American commissioners epitomized, the Americans demonstrated the art of compromise, but what they yielded was trivial while they remained adamant on the crucial issues—obtaining absolute independence and a continental domain for thirteen littoral states. For a perspicuity spiced with audacity, for a tenacity tempered by flexibility, a free people is eternally in their debt.

NOTES TO CHAPTER III

1. *Histoire de la Participation de la France a l'établissement des États-Unis d'Amérique* (5 vols., Paris, 1886–1892).

2. Richard W. Van Alstyne, *Empire and Independence: The International History of the American Revolution* (New York, 1965), p. 133.

3. Force, *Amer. Arch.*, 4th ser., II, 1866–1869.

4. Thomas Jefferson to John Randolph, Aug. 25, 1775. *Jefferson Papers* (Boyd, ed.), I, 240–243.

5. *Marginal Comment in an Inquiry into the Nature and Causes of the Present Disputes* (London, 1769), quoted by

Verner W. Crane, "Certain Writings of Benjamin Franklin on the British Empire and the American Colonies," in Bibliographical Society of America, *Papers,* XXVIII, Pt. 1 (1934), 23n.

6. See Gerald Stourzh, *Benjamin Franklin and American Foreign Policy* (Chicago, 1954), pp. 123–126.

7. Journal of Arthur Lee, Nov. 27, 1777. In R. H. Lee, *Life of Arthur Lee,* I, 354–358.

8. Stevens Facsimiles, Nos. 1316, 1319, 1332.

9. Hamilton to William Duer, May 6, 1777. Hamilton Papers, 1st ser., Library of Congress.

10. Gouverneur Morris Papers, Columbia University Libraries. The postscript was deleted from the letter as published in Jared Sparks, *The Life of Gouverneur Morris* (Boston, 1832), I, 172, 173. The textual variations in the Fitzpatrick edition, *Writings of George Washington,* XII, 226–227, are attributed to the fact that the letter therein published came from a letterbook copy printed in the W. C. Ford edition.

11. Van Alstyne, *op. cit.,* p. 133.

12. Jefferson to Lee, Aug. 30; Lee to Jefferson, Oct. 5, 1778. *Jefferson Papers,* II, 210–211, 214–216.

13. Vergennes' views on the rival fisheries' claims are treated sympathetically most recently by Orville T. Murphy, "The Comte de Vergennes, the Newfoundland Fisheries, and the Peace Negotiations of 1783: A Reconsideration," *Canadian Historical Rev.,* XLVI (1965), 32–46.

14. William Eden, *Four Letters to the Earl of Carlisle* (Edinburgh, 1779).

15. R. B. Morris, *The Peacemakers: The Great Powers and American Independence* (New York, 1965).

IV

CONFEDERATION
AND
CONSTITUTION

Fulfillment or
Counterrevolution?

In considering the War for Independence as in fact two revolutions historians have all agreed that it was initially a war for liberation from the bonds of imperial control. Some have also chosen to regard it as a catalyst to social change at home, and still others as an internal struggle for power between "radicals" and "conservatives," culminating in the adoption of the Constitution, which amounted to a *coup d'état*. This critical view of the tactics and goals of the Founding Fathers we normally associate with the historians of the Populist-Progressive era, whose alienation from the business society of their generation was indisputably more profound than that of historians of our own day.

The notion that the American Revolution constituted an internal power struggle was by no means a novel one even at the beginning of the present century, but in 1909 the talented and perceptive Carl Becker published a seminal Ph.D. thesis entitled *The History of Political Parties in the Province of New York, 1760–1776*. Confining himself to this one colony, Becker viewed the war as being waged therein to decide not only home rule but who should rule at home. In a generalized form his thesis was expanded a few years later by Arthur Schlesinger, Sr., who, in his *Colonial Merchants and the American Revolution*, documented an interesting struggle for pre-Revolutionary leadership waged in the leading colonial towns between the conservative merchants and the lower-class radicals. The former, buttressed by superb legal talent, gave the initial thrust to the Revolutionary protest against England's trade and revenue measures, but the latter, to the merchants' consternation, crowded in, accelerating the engine of violence, and in fact taking over the Revolutionary machinery.

Drawing essentially upon these two specialized studies, later historians have generalized that it was the radicals who seized the Revolutionary helm and pressed the country into war, while the conservatives among the Patriots plotted to win back their ancient control. These revisionist historians argue that the Articles of Confederation were the constitutional expression of this allegedly democratic movement, and the Constitution in effect was a counterrevolution.[1]

That deep cleavage which exists between historical schools over whether or not the Confederation interlude was truly critical or whether or not a counterrevolution took place springs from a sharp divergence in interpreting the American Revolution and the issues over which it was waged. The Antifederalist school of historiography sees the Patriots divided on the eve of the Revolution between a "radical" and a "conservative" party. The former comprised the town masses and frontier settlers. The radicals, according to the Antifederalist historians, fought for an internal revolution; the conservatives, who were, it goes without saying, the affluent, allowed themselves to be reluctantly dragged into the war, and sought merely independence from England; otherwise they acted in defense of the *status quo.*

In this version there seems to be little or no room for Tories, for Redcoats, or for Hessians. This formula fails to explain why New York City and Philadelphia were hotbeds of loyalism, why the Regulators of Carolina and the levelers of upstate New York numbered so many Tories, or why debtors and creditors, hard-money men and paper-money men, suffrage expansionists and suffrage restrictionists were arrayed on the same side. It fails to explain the prominent role of the Whig conservative élite in bringing about the Revolution or to lay the foundation for understanding why in so many areas the radicalism of the leadership was that of the Gironde, not the Mountain.[2]

So much of the argument since Carl Becker's day turns on the analysis of the radical party—its organization, composition, and goals—that the historian has no choice but to examine this specimen under the microscope and to ascertain just what is happening to the cells. To Becker, the town mechanics embodied the concept of Revolutionary democracy; their extralegal committees, contributing to Revolutionary tension by both propaganda and action, provided an "open door" through which the politically excluded thrust themselves into the arena of politics. Through that door, according to Becker, it was "the unfranchised mechanic and artisan" above all who strode.

In stressing the so-called lower-class elements behind radical activities Becker foreshadowed the more recent emphasis of historians like George Rudé, Albert Soboul, and Robert R. Palmer, among others, on the role of the mob, the crowd, the unskilled laborers, and the mechanics in contemporary European movements of reform and revolution. In both England and France, but notably in the former country, middle-class reformers exploited "mobs" to pressure governing groups into making changes; in turn the mobs might well have propelled the middle-class reformers in directions more extreme than they would have moved if such demonstrations had not taken place. One must remember, though, that mobbism is no synonym for liberal reform, and that mobs could at times be moved by extremely reactionary impulses. Witness the outrageous Gordon Riots in England during the June days of 1780, when the lowest elements, aroused by upper-class agitators, sought to compel by violent civil disorder the repeal of laws extending a measure of religious toleration to Catholics. In America, after 1764, mobs demonstrated with precise objects in mind. They set up liberty poles, sacked the mansions of obnoxious royal officials, and, with the coming of war, tarred and feathered suspected Loyalists and threatened the lives of profiteers.

The nucleus of such radical mob action was the Sons of Liberty, groups first making their appearance in New England and New York, but soon springing up in virtually every colonial town. These organizations functioned as independent entities and in fact no one has demonstrated a clear and undisputed lineage between them and the far more effective committees of correspondence. In New York the initial impetus for the movement seems to have been provided by relatively conservative lawyers of the stature of William Livingston, John Morin Scott, and the later Tory William Smith, and the direct hand in organizing such groups was assumed by wealthy merchants like Isaac Sears, John Lamb, and Alexander McDougall.

True, both the agitating lawyers and the agitating merchants might be distinguished on some issues from their professional and business associates. The lawyers often belonged to that Presbyterian wing that had fought the inroads of the Anglican establishment in New York, while the merchants were chiefly new men, not boasting ties to long-established mercantile families. Still, in the nature of their legal practice or in the patterns of their trade there was little or nothing to distinguish them from other affluent lawyers and businessmen in New York.

At the heart of such radical demonstrations was the "mechanic," a catchall term covering both master employers and journeymen wage workers. In that ambivalent sense "mechanic" continues in common use well into the Confederation period, although by the national era the term takes on a more distinctly proletarian character. One thing is clear. The "mechanics" were the "radicals" and as such were indispensable ingredients in fueling the flame of political protest.

What complicates the problem in New York, however, is the fact that the aristocratic political leadership, divided in the province between the Livingston and De Lancey family factions, overtly courted such popular support, and, to compound the confusion, the De Lanceys, the party ultimately tainted with Toryism, seemed much more active in the radical protest movements of 1765 and 1768 than did the Livingstons.

The older view that the right to vote in the colonies was severely circumscribed by property qualifications has been pretty thoroughly discredited in recent years.[3] New York City is a case in point. What makes that city so sensitive a barometer of mass opinion in this period is the fact that the franchise therein was especially liberal, and that an overwhelming majority of adult males were enabled to vote by the eve of the Revolution.[4] It was one thing to possess the franchise; it was quite another to take full advantage of that right. In New York it is apparent that the lower-class groups failed to develop political leaders of their own either in the city or in the province, but rather meekly obeyed the aristocratic politicians who had proved themselves so adept at manipulating votes and opinion. Furthermore, as a formal organization the Sons of Liberty had a relatively short life, leaving its chief agitators to conduct operations largely on their own.[5]

Much has been made of the fact that during the protests over the Stamp Act certain working-class elements advocated that trade be carried on without stamps in opposition to the radical merchants, who espoused a boycott on imports. It is significant that the merchants won the day. Differences in tactics between the various radical elements were bound to crop up from time to time, but evidence is lacking that the working class existed as an independent force in the pre-Revolutionary period. Seamen and roustabouts in seaport towns like New York or Providence allowed themselves to be manipulated by shipowners and ship captains, and mechanics followed the lead of the radical merchants.[6] It must be remembered, too, that the "Sons of Liberty" covered a variety of protest groups, by no means of proletarian origin. Thomas Hutchinson, for example, recounts some liberty business at Cambridge, Massachusetts, where Harvard College undergraduates protested compulsory chapel attendance and the regulation of the tutors not to excuse students before prayers or college exercises. The scholars assembled in a body around a great tree, to which they gave the name "the tree of liberty," and denounced the rule of the tutors as "unconstitutional." Some rioting ensued, with broken windows and brickbats hurled into rooms occupied by the tutors. The overseers stood firm, the ringleaders were expelled, and the rank and file yielded to authority. Almost at the very moment that this demonstration was taking place at Cambridge an assemblage of more proletarian origin was being mustered across the Charles and proceeded to hang a stuffed dummy representing one of the inspectors of customs to a Liberty Tree in Boston, while mobs, protesting the Townshend Acts, rallied before the province house and threatened the governor.[7] In this fashion the contagion of liberty spread among all classes, manifesting itself in quite diverse ways.

The substance of recent findings underscores the failure of radical groups in the pre-Revolutionary period to unite on goals, and reveals that such divisions continued after the start of the war. For example, the radicals in Dutchess County, New York, split with the New York City radicals over taxation. The former favored avoiding tax burdens by securing needed revenue from the confiscation of Loyalist estates; the latter, both during and after the war, advocated adequate taxation to enable the state to meet its obligations to Congress. Again, one finds that the New York City radicals united with the rest of the business community in the Confederation period in advocating measures to strengthen federalism. Furthermore, no clear line of continuity between the Sons of Liberty and the later Antifederalists can be demonstrated. With the exception of John Lamb, all the old Sons of Liberty remained steadfastly Federalist, and the mechanics of New York City sent to the state's ratifying convention none other than such arch-Federalist conservatives as John Jay, Robert R. Livingston, and James Duane. The mechanics, indeed, not only supported the Constitution but supported it fervently.[8]

In this alignment of erstwhile urban radicals with the conservative supporters of the Federal Constitution, New York City was by no means atypical. In postwar Charleston the mechanics joined with the merchants in moves to expel the Tories or prevent their return, only to be resisted bitterly by that old Liberty Boy Christopher Gadsden. In this Southern seaport, as in New York City, it is possible to discover certain issues dividing the mechanic-merchant combinations from the conservative planters, but despite such divisions the Charleston mechanics at the state's ratifying convention of 1788 voted "yes" on the issue of the new Constitution. In fact, in all the leading towns the mechanics played a conspicuous part in the celebrations that took place when each state in turn ratified the Constitution.[9] Little or no support can be found, it seems, for those who would press the Becker thesis and establish a line of continuity between the prewar radicalism of the so-called working-class elements and the Antifederalism of the Confederation period. Nor has anyone been successful in establishing a link between the conservatism of pre-Revolutionary years and that counterrevolution alleged to have taken place in the Confederation period.

Marxist historians are invariably confounded when they encounter evidence showing that on certain issues the classic class conflict is not applicable, but that, to the contrary, workingmen and their employers might share the same political views when economic and ideological interests are not in collision. In the modern world nationalism has proved to be a more pervasive force than proletarian identity. So many supporting illustrations come to mind since 1914 that the point hardly needs belaboring, but the contemporary reader might well be reminded that when the militant Maritime Union pickets foreign ships whose companies do business with North Vietnam they are scarcely showing solidarity with the May 2nd movement.

The thesis that the Constitution amounted to a counterrevolution, a repudiation of the goals of the Great Declaration, was fashionable in the generation of postwar and depression. To support the argument that the affluent conspired and the poor were subverted one had to be willing not only to generalize from the local, the particular, and the exceptional, but also to posit a drastically revisionist view of the historiography of the Confederation period. One had to be prepared to paint in roseate hues a period of American history traditionally depicted as an epoch in governmental futility, when this nation's very existence was threatened by divisive forces within and a hostile world without.

Now, historians of all schools recognize that the Revolution did not end with the signing of the Definitive Treaty of Paris on September 3, 1783, that enemy troops still had to be evacuated, the West had to be secured, the nation's economy had to be rebuilt after eight years of often savage warfare and widespread plunder, and the new government which had been set up under the Articles of Confederation had to be put to the tests of peacetime operation.

The revisionists have raised basic questions and are entitled to informed replies. Was the Confederation a success and did the Constitution result from a paranoid view of American trends held by certain conservatives, or had that government in fact broken down and were those who supplanted the old Articles by the Constitution entitled to be considered the saviors of their country rather than the conspirators against its liberties? One would think these should be simple questions to answer. Alas, they were not that simple to contemporaries, nor are they that simple today. Measuring the effectiveness of a political apparatus, a subjective matter at best, requires in this instance testing at two levels, that of the Confederation and that of the separate states, and it is not impossible that one will come up with contradictory findings; appraising the functioning of the economy in that relatively remote period presents enormous difficulties. Just consider how almost totally lacking the period under review is in compilations of reliable statistical data or in economic indices available in such rich profusion for those who would diagnose our present economy. The subject abounds in one pitfall after another. Potential military and diplomatic hazards are at best conjectural, and the psychological climate in which the new nationalism could thrive might well vary from region to region and from person to person.

In fact, the two opposing views of the post-Revolutionary years which are held by historians of the twentieth century can be traced directly to the Founding Fathers. The first, the approach of Washington, Madison, and Hamilton, was accepted by most historians of the post-Revolutionary generation, and developed by George Bancroft, John Fiske, John B. McMaster, and with some reservations by Andrew C. McLaughlin. The other is the approach of certain Antifederalist leaders, a road to be traversed by Henry B. Dawson, by J. Allen Smith, by the early Charles A. Beard, and by his more recent disciples.

If one could read the minds of the majority of the Founding Fathers in 1787—and an abundant and ever-increasing quantity of firsthand documentation makes this a less formidable effort than it seems on its face—one might be very much surprised indeed that any issue should have arisen in historiography about the years of the Confederation. The majority of the Founders saw a clear drift toward anarchy culminating in a crisis. Constantly needled by such correspondents as Henry Knox and David Humphreys, Washington was alarmed at the weaknesses of the Confederacy, an alarm intensified as the disorders in Massachusetts in the fall of 1786 seemed to portend a crisis for the nation. "I predict the worst consequences from a half-starved, limping government, always moving upon crutches and tottering at every step," he wrote. On August 1, 1786, he asserted: "I do not conceive we can long exist as a nation without having lodged somewhere a power which will pervade the whole Union in as energetic a manner as the authority of the State governments extends over the several states." On October 22nd he wrote David Humphreys: "But for God's sake tell me what is the cause of all these commotions? . . . I am mortified beyond expression that in the moment of our acknowledged independence we should by our conduct verify the predictions of our transatlantic foe, and render ourselves ridiculous and contemptible in the eyes of all Europe." Nine days later he wrote Henry Lee: "To be more exposed in the eyes of the world, and more contemptible than we already are, is hardly possible."[10] On November 5th he told James Madison that "We are fast verging to anarchy and confusion!"[11]

Others than the New England Federalists, who were closest to Shays' Rebellion and understandably perturbed, shared Washington's views about the state of the nation. Henry Lee declared: "We are all in dire apprehension that a beginning of anarchy with all its calamitys has approached, and have no means to stop the dreadful work."[12] In December of 1786 Madison wrote Jefferson of "dangerous defects" in the Confederation.[13] During the fall of 1786 John Jay kept writing Jefferson that "the inefficacy of our Government becomes daily more and more apparent" and intimated that the Shaysites had more "extensive" objectives than the immediate redress of grievances.[14] Edmund Randolph, who oscillated between federalism and Antifederalism, wrote Washington in March of 1787, "Every day brings forth some new crisis"; and he expressed doubt whether Congress could survive beyond the current year.[15] No one at the Constitutional Convention was more explicit than Randolph in spelling out the defects of the government, which he considered "totally inadequate to the peace, safety, and security of the Confederation" and which he repeatedly denounced for its "imbecility."[16]

For the classic contemporary view of the alarming weaknesses of the Confederation we must turn to *The Federalist*. Therein Hamilton, a consistent viewer-with-alarm during this period, attacks the Confederation government as inefficient, asserts that the country had "reached almost the last stage of national humiliation," speaks disparagingly of "the present shadow of a federal government," views the Confederacy as dying, and urges ratification of the Constitution to prevent anarchy, civil war, and "perhaps the military despotism of a victorious demagogue."[17] It would be easy to pile up assertions in similar vein from the pens of Knox and the two Morrises.

These Federalist worthies were in general agreement that the weaknesses of the Confederation could be attributed to financial muddling by the states; to English dumping; to the loss of the British West Indian market; to paper money; to stay laws; to state tariffs; but, above all, to a lack of coercive power by a central authority. Observers in charge of foreign affairs, notably John Jay and John Adams, felt that this was the most critical spot in the American system of government. "I may reason till I die to no purpose," declared Adams in June, 1785. "It is unanimity in America which will produce a fair treaty of commerce."[18]

Still, though in eloquence, prestige, and even in numbers among the leadership the Federalist view of conditions had impressive support, it was far from universally held. George Clinton, the *bête noire* of the nationalist leaders, was quoted as intimating that the calling of a Constitutional Convention was "calculated to impress the people with an idea of evils which do not exist."[19] At the convention, Gunning Bedford of Delaware expressed a complacent view of the government of the Confederacy, and at the Pennsylvania ratifying convention Antifederalists under the leadership of William Findley, Robert Whitehill, and John Smilie asserted that the people along with the legislature had been frightened into consenting to a state convention by unfounded talk of impending anarchy.

Thus, there was a division of opinion in 1787 about conditions in the Confederation, and there never has ceased to be down to the present day. More recent writers who look at the Confederation through Antifederalist spectacles are buoyed up by the fact that Franklin and Jefferson were not as disturbed about conditions as other contemporaries. Yet Jefferson, as he was passing through Boston on his way to France, found "the conviction growing strongly that nothing could preserve the confederacy unless the bond of union, their common council, should be strengthened."[20] It is perhaps especially significant that when Franklin, Jefferson, and Robert R. Livingston expressed in writing a more roseate view of conditions than other Founding Fathers, they were making these observations to foreigners—to Frenchmen or to Englishmen. They were seeking to reassure friends and well-wishers of America abroad that this country was not headed for a collapse. Such assertions must be discounted as skillful propaganda. In France, for example, Jefferson reassured Démeunier that the United States was in no danger of bankruptcy and that, with certain minor exceptions, "the Confederation is a wonderfully perfect instrument."[21] Similarly, when Franklin wrote to M. Le Veillard on March 6, 1786, that "America never was in higher prosperity,"[22] commodity prices had steadily dropped—they were to decline 30 percent between 1785 and 1789; farm wages were shrinking and were to fall to a low of forty cents a day by 1787; mortgage foreclosures and judgments for debts in central and western Massachusetts had reached an all-time high; and in the Valley of Virginia, as Freeman Hart has pointed out, executions more than doubled between 1784 and 1788.[23] In fact, the only economic index that showed an upturn was that for foreign trade, for in commerce the worst of the depression set in a bit earlier than in other lines and showed a more complete recovery by 1788. Again, when Livingston wrote Lafayette in April, 1787, that commodity prices and wages were higher than before the war he was evading the real issue of how far they had dropped since the coming of the peace.[24]

Even the younger generation, men who could scarcely be accused of strong Federalist attachments, accepted the Federalist view of the glaring weaknesses of the Confederation. Consider, for example, Andrew Jackson, who was admitted to practice law the year the Constitutional Convention met in Philadelphia. In 1832 he publicly subscribed to the views incorporated in the draft of the Proclamation against Nullification which was prepared by that distinguished jurist, Secretary of State Edward Livingston, himself a few years the President's senior. The Proclamation declared: "But the defects of the Confederation need not be detailed. Under its operation we could scarcely be called a nation. We had neither prosperity at home nor consideration abroad. This state of things could not be endured, and our present happy Constitution was formed, but formed in vain if this fatal doctrine prevails."[25]

Jackson's view of the Confederation period was endorsed by the nationalist commentators on the Constitution and by the nationalist historians. It was expounded by James Wilson and Nathaniel Chipman, by Nathan Dane, and most notably by Joseph Story and George Ticknor Curtis, who gave formal expression to the views of Daniel Webster. In his *History of the Origin, Formation, and Adoption of the Constitution,* first published in 1854, Curtis begins by declaring: "The Constitution of the United States was the means by which republican liberty was saved from the consequences of impending anarchy." Paraphrasing the Founding Fathers, Curtis saw the Confederation as "a great shadow without the substance of a government." He depicted the whole period as replete with "dangers and difficulties," full of "suffering and peril."[26]

Curtis' view of the Confederation interlude was fully shared by the nationalist historians writing in the generation or two following the adoption of the Constitution. Most distinguished of this group, George Bancroft, put off writing about the post-Revolutionary era until the closing years of his life. His *History of the Formation of the Constitution of the United States of America* was not published until 1882. As might be expected, Bancroft viewed the period from a nationalist or continental point of view. He stressed the "helplessness" of Congress, whose "perpetual failures" he considered "inherent and incurable." To Bancroft "no ray of hope remained" but from the convention summoned at Annapolis.[27]

Perhaps the historian who coined the term "critical period" to describe the Confederation interlude was William Henry Trescot. In his rather temperate and fairminded *Diplomatic History of the Administrations of Washington and Adams,* published in 1857, he asserted: "Indeed, it would be more correct to say, that the most critical period of the country's history embraced the time between the peace of 1783 and the adoption of the constitution in 1788."[28] This point of view was adopted by Frothingham, by Schouler, and by von Holst. The last-named spoke of "the contemptible impotence of Congress." This was strong language, but Washington had used it before him.[29]

The classic exposition of the Federalist approach is found in John Fiske's *The Critical Period in American History 1783–1789*. His title has fastened upon an epoch in American history a popular nomenclature that dies hard. The first edition appeared in 1888, not too long after the appearance of Bancroft's *Last Revision*. The title and theme of the book were suggested by the fact of Tom Paine's stopping the publication of the "Crisis," on hearing the news of the treaty of peace in 1783. Now, Paine said, "the times that tried men's souls are over." Fiske does not agree with Paine. The next five years, he contends, were to be the most critical time of all. Fiske used the term "critical" first to settle the question whether there was to be a national government or a group of small city-states. Secondly, he used the term to describe what he regarded to be the utter incompetence of the states and the federal government to deal with the problem of post-war reconstruction. To Fiske the drift "toward anarchy" was only checked by the eleventh-hour ratification of the Federal Constitution.[30] John Fiske's approach to the era had an enormous impact both upon the public and upon fellow historians. John Bach McMaster adopts it without reservations,[31] and Andrew C. McLaughlin, though with some qualifications regarding the extent of the trade depression.[32]

The Antifederalist or prodemocratic interpretation (and it is hardly necessary to point out that the two terms are not necessarily equated) was perhaps first, among nineteenth-century historians, expounded by Henry B. Dawson, a learned military historian of the American Revolution, who also devoted himself to studying the role of the masses in that war and had a penchant for picking controversial issues which he fought with relish and passion. In an article in the *Historical Magazine* in 1871, Dawson attempted to refute John Lothrop Motley, who, in a celebrated letter to the London *Times* written during the Civil War, had asserted that the Confederation was a period of "chaos," in which the absence of law, order, and security for life and property was "as absolute as could be well conceived in a civilized land." These were reckless and false accusations, Dawson charged. He traced their origin to distinguished men of the Confederation period who had spread them "for selfish or partisan motives." He accused these leaders of having "nullified the established law of the Confederacy and violently and corruptly substituted for it what they styled the Constitution of the

United States." Dawson had made extreme and curiously unbalanced charges but failed to substantiate them. The significance of the attack, however, lies far less in the kind of evidence adduced than in its formulation of the notion that the Federalists conspired to falsify the true conditions of the period in a deliberate effort to create panic and undermine the government of the Confederation. Oddly enough, the criminal statistics Dawson cites for New York State not only are inconclusive regarding lawlessness but point directly opposite to what Dawson believed. They indicate that in New York City and County there were almost twice as many indictments between 1784 and 1789 as there were for the first five years under the new federal government.[33] Concerning law and order, Dawson may very well have been on the right track, but somewhere along the path he lost the scent.

Despite the intemperate character of his attack, Dawson had touched off certain doubts as to the reportorial objectivity both of the Founding Fathers and of later historians. These were again raised in 1907, when J. Allen Smith, in his *The Spirit of American Government,* attacked on a second front, contending that the Constitution was the result of a counterrevolution. To him the Declaration of Independence spelled sweeping changes in the American form of government, changes manifest in an omnipotent legislature and the overthrow of the system of checks and balances which had been derived from the English constitution, with its characteristic blending of monarchical, aristocratic, and democratic elements. To Smith the chief feature of the Articles of Confederation was the entire absence of checks and balances, the vesting of all power in a single legislative body, unchecked by a distinct executive or judiciary. The fact that the power which was vested in the continental legislature was ineffectual did not disturb him. His main point, though, was that such democratic changes had been wrought by radical forces and that the conservatives, once they had a chance to assess the situation, set about, in more or less conspiratorial fashion, to redress the balance. The Constitutional Convention was called, according to Smith, not only to impart vigor to the government but to institute an elaborate system of constitutional checks. The adoption of this system he calls a "triumph of a skillfully directed reactionary movement."[34] The idea that the adoption of the Constitution was the result of a struggle among interest groups was pressed by Arthur F. Bentley in *The Process of Government* (1908), in language which stemmed from Madison's *Federalist 10,* and in a more naked form by A. M. Simons' *Social Forces in American History* (1911).

The most significant amplification of the Smith-Bentley-Simons approach came in 1913 from the pen of Charles A. Beard. In his *An Economic Interpretation of the Constitution of the United States* Beard concedes that "interpretive schools seem always to originate in social antagonism," but he prefers the road which explains proximate or remote causes and relations to the so-called "impartial" history which surveys outward events and classifies and orders phenomena.[35] Beard was profoundly influenced by Frederick Jackson Turner, who substituted for the states' rights interpretation of our history a recognition of social and economic areas, independent of state lines, which acted as units in political history. For the period of the Confederation the most important Turnerian contribution was Orin G. Libby's *Geographical Distribution of the Vote of the Thirteen States on the Federal Constitution,* an original and searching study published as far back as 1894. Beard found that nationalism cut across state lines, that it was created by a welding of economic interests of creditors, holders of personalty—especially public securities—manufacturers, shippers, commercial groups, and speculators in Western lands. While this majestic formula helped explain why people were Federalists, it has failed dismally in explaining differences between Federalists and Antifederalists.

Beard suggested that general social conditions were prosperous and that the defects of the Articles did not justify the "loud complaints" of the advocates of change. In short, Beard found that the "critical period" was really not so critical after all, but, drawing upon Dawson's article, "a phantom of the imagination produced by some undoubted evils which could have been remedied without a political revolution."[36] Save for a quotation from Franklin, Beard fails to document this crucial generalization.

Lest anyone should carry away with him the view that Beard opposed the Constitution, as did J. Allen Smith, it might be well to point out that in his *Supreme Court and the Constitution,* published the previous year, he praised the Constitution and furnished historical precedents for judicial review. In later years he drew further and further away from any monolithic economic interpretation of the period. Although his *Rise of American Civilization* adhered to the approach of his *Economic Interpretation,* as did Parrington's treatment in *Main Currents in American Thought,* Beard by 1935 completely repudiated economic determinism. In *The Republic* (1943) he considered the adoption of the Constitution as the alternative to military dictatorship. In his *Basic History of the United States* (1944) he defended checks and balances as curbs on despotic powers, whereas in his earlier *Rise of American Civilization* he insisted that checks and balances dissolved "the energy of the democratic majority."[37] In *The Enduring Federalist,* published in 1948, he refers to the Congress of the Confederation as "a kind of debating society" and describes conditions in the Confederation period in language which would have gratified Fiske and perhaps shocked Bancroft.[38] In short, by the end of his career, Beard, the confirmed nationalist and isolationist, had moved a long way from the Beard of pre-World War I days.

It is the unreconstructed Beard who captured the imagination of pre-Space Age scholars. Professor Merrill Jensen, to cite a leading exemplar, expounds learnedly and at length the argument that the Federalist party was organized to destroy the kind of democratic government and economic practice made possible by the Articles of Confederation.[39] Jensen sees the Articles as a constitutional expression of the philosophy of the Declaration of Independence, the Constitution as a betrayal of those principles. To Jensen the Articles were designed to prevent the central government from infringing upon the rights of the states, whereas the Constitution was designed to check both the states and the democracy that found expression within state bounds. As Jensen sees it, the Confederation government went amiss, not because it was inadequate but because the radicals failed to maintain the organization they had created to bring about the American Revolution. He speaks of the radicals as having won *"their war,"* but the fact remains that it was as much the war of the conservatives; probably a good deal more so.

The revisionists of the Beard-Jensen school are perhaps most effective in recounting the constructive steps taken in the Confederation period to repair federal and state finances. They show that the Confederation actually managed to reduce the principal of its debt, and praise the states for their role in paying the national debt. They point to the rapid amortization of state debts as evidence of the ability of the states to put their financial houses in order without much help from a central government. There is no doubt whatsoever that the states had now largely assumed the debt-funding function that the federal government had proved incapable of shouldering.[40] But in terms of more recent ideas of economic planning it would now seem that states like Massachusetts made the mistake of too rapidly amortizing the state debt, thereby initiating a sharp deflationary thrust. Even a conservative like Governor Bowdoin urged in 1786 a more gradual plan of amortization than that which the property-conscious legislature had enacted.

In short, the Beardian approach has served to present the Confederation period in a more constructive light, to give greater recognition to signs of economic expansion in the period and to the stabilizing role of the states, particularly in financial matters. As Allan Nevins pointed out long before Jensen, when the new federal government went into effect, in no state was the debt appallingly high, and in some it was already low.[41] Mr. Jensen is doubtless correct in arguing that in most states the forces of law and order never lost the upper hand. In New York that arch-Antifederalist George Clinton personally led the troops of the state against the insurrectionary Shays. In most cases —and Maryland is an excellent example—the disgruntled elements confined their efforts to obtaining relief in a legal manner through legislative action.

When the Antifederalists turn from the states to the federal government, they stand on less solid ground. In order to bolster their arguments that the Confederation was a viable instrument and that it was snuffed out by conspiracy the revisionists need to demonstrate, first, that there was a consistent struggle between republicans and nationalists throughout the whole period, 1776–1789, and, second, that a counterrevolution by conservatives occurred during some stage of the Confederation. A defense of either position rests upon an enormously oversimplified view of factions, sections, and individual motivations. To assert both can only be done if one is predisposed to find conspiracy and betrayal in all the actions of those men who, as Hamilton so felicitously phrased it, "think continentally," while at the same time one must be prepared to find the extreme particularists and states'-

righters of the George Clinton stripe possessing a monopoly of republican virtue and a selfless dedication to the public good. Finally, the burden of proof rests upon the Antifederalist revisionists to show that the years 1785–1787 were not "critical" as regards the economy, the nation's fiscal position, and its diplomatic posture.

Let us consider each in turn. It would be helpful to the revisionist cause if one could discern a consistent struggle being waged between republicans and nationalists during the period 1776–1789, and at least one recent writer sees the epoch in such broad outline.[42] Easterners and Southerners, united in their staunch republicanism, are portrayed as sharing various personality traits in common, as being strait-laced about sex and recognizing the line of conflict-of-interest between private gain and public mission. Contrariwise, their opponents, the nationalists, as they appear on this canvas, are shown to be downright immoral, robust if not lusty, cynical about the rights of man, and insensitive to conflict-of-interest. Often educated abroad and rooted primarily in the Middle States and South Carolina, these commercially minded cosmopolites had bold financial plans and needed a strong nation to give them reality. Provocative as this alignment of groups by interest and temperament may well be, it fails to take into account a multitude of exceptions. By this formula how does one explain that conservative nationalist John Dickinson, who authored the states' rights Articles of Confederation, or the New England Puritan John Adams, who bristled at the hint of speculation yet believed devoutly in balanced government, and his fellow nationalist John Jay, who after being hailed as the darling of the pro-French conservatives in Congress became the hero of the Lee-Adams isolationist circle? And where does it place George Washington, a statesman who embodied all the republican virtues of Cato the Elder, was consistently prominent as a nationalist, and yet with equal consistency avowed his faith in the supremacy of civilian over military rule?

"Counterrevolution," when used for the Confederation period, is a pejorative term describing a gradual change in the psychological climate, a change reflected to some extent in the rise and decline of factions in Congress and in an upthrust of conservative forces in the states. The conspiratorial overtones and forceful take-over that the term suggests are melodramatic shadings contributed by supersensitive historians who have been ready to find conspiracy under every bed in every Philadelphia lodging house which was host to Congressional delegates, merchants, or financiers.

Whatever impulse for change or take-over did materialize was inspired by the financial needs of the nation and whatever chance there might have been for a military coup to effect such changes was dissipated when the nation managed to ride out the financial storms of the years 1781–1783. E. James Ferguson, in his valuable study, *The Power of the Purse*, has given us the most suggestive documentation for these critical years.

The events leading to a proposed take-over came about innocently enough. Americans had fought a revolution against increasing centralizing trends from a distant government, and most Patriots were unprepared to replace the old British Empire with a strong central government in America. The Articles of Confederation reflected this states' rights temper. Patriots realized that a weak central government would be a handicap to waging all-out war, but accepted it as a calculated risk. The extent of that risk was perhaps not fully appreciated, however, until the year 1779, by which time the inflationary spiral took off in earnest. When Congress decided to stop further emissions of paper money it publicly confessed that it had exhausted this stopgap financial resource which it had failed to buttress by securing the power to tax. The decision exposed to full view the grave weakness of Congress under the Articles of Confederation. Now even old-line radicals began to speak less about liberty and more about the need for financial stability and strong government. Soon conservative majorities controlled the legislatures of states like Massachusetts, Pennsylvania, and Virginia, and new delegates altered the composition of Congress, giving to both Northern and Southern delegations a somewhat conservative coloration. Even Sam Adams conceded that practical affairs sometimes required actions not described in the "political catechisms" of good republicans.[43]

The nation's fiscal collapse triggered a cluster of measures transcending fiscal reform and aimed at recasting the structure of the Union. Young Alexander Hamilton had even anticipated the prime movers, but the architect of the new edifice was the financier Robert Morris, aided and abetted by his associate, Gouverneur Morris. In a far-reaching design for his Bank of North America Morris embraced the intention of bringing about an early retirement of all federal and state currencies and replacing them with bank notes, and, as he explained in a letter to John Jay, penned in July of 1781, with the purpose of uniting "the several States more closely together in one general money connexion, and indissolubly to attach many powerful individuals to the cause of our country by the strong principle of self-love and the immediate sense of private interest."[44] As superintendent of finance Morris accomplished a good deal. He introduced the contract system of supplying the army. He effected necessary economies in the federal budget, and his bank provided the flexibility necessary to underwrite his complex fiscal operations. Perhaps ambitious ideas of political change lurked behind his fiscal goals. The record is murky, but we do know that about Morris there soon arose a group of nationalists who insisted that the debts, both state and federal, should be paid only out of federal taxes, levied and collected by Congress. This objective would necessitate amending the Articles to provide Congress with the taxing power it lacked.

Whatever Morris' long-term goals, his short-run plans went awry. Rhode Island, albeit from motives of special interest, refused to grant to Congress the power to levy an impost. Morris' response was a dramatic protest of resignation of his post as superintendent of finance. He would not proceed further to increase the debt while the prospect of paying it diminished. He would never, he asserted, "be the minister of injustice."[45] If Morris' strategy was to force Congress into assuming an aggressive posture by venturing to exercise implied powers under the Confederation to levy taxes, it failed of its purpose.

With Congress supine if not inert, the initiative was seized by a group of discontented army officers who had gone without pay for a painful stretch of time. The hand of the Morris coterie was seen in the inner circle of army conservatives, which included Richard Peters, the head of the Board of War, the archnationalist Alexander Hamilton, and that ex-Son of Liberty General Alexander McDougall. Their ultimate aims are shadowy but we would now say that they sought what would have amounted to a *coup d'état* inside the framework of the Articles of Confederation. In combination with the public creditors the army officers constituted a formidable group. What added to the complexity of the picture and compounds its inconsistency was the alleged role in the plot of General Horatio Gates, that darling of the old republican faction. Opposed to them all, friend and old foe alike, stood George Washington, whose very name had been anathema to the virtuous Lee-Adams republicans. Yet it was Washington who refused to put military pressure on Congress or to lead a thinly veiled military coup. It was he who courageously disavowed the Newburgh plot and rebuked the plotters. And that was the end of it. Disappointed in their hopes of achieving a settlement through Congress, the creditors now looked to the states for the satisfaction of their claims, and the conspiracy against the Confederation, if it ever really existed, dissolved.

The ability of the country to function fiscally thereafter, however, should not blind us to the fiscal impotence of Congress. While the states now proceeded to assume a goodly part of the domestic burden of debt, Congress, confronted with the claims of foreign nations and foreign creditors, was obliged to default on its foreign obligations in large part. After 1785 Congress failed to pay interest on its Dutch loan, and it defaulted entirely on the contracts made with the French government. In effect, by the year 1787 the national credit had virtually vanished and Congress was teetering on the brink of bankruptcy. Critical though the moment, the state of New York, which was enjoying considerable revenue from its own imposts, in substance refused to concur in a new proposal to grant the taxing power to Congress, very much as had Rhode Island some years before.

Even old republicans like Arthur and Richard Henry Lee now appeared converted by the solid arguments presented some years before by Robert Morris as to the need for granting to Congress the power to tax, and David Howell of Rhode Island, who had been accused of wrecking Congress's fiscal program back in 1782, was to move into the Federalist camp. On the crucial issue of the taxing power and control over commerce virtually all public-spirited men in America were in agreement: the Articles must be changed. In short, the move to establish the Constitution was not a conspiracy of the moneyed interests but a broad-bottomed movement, reaching down to the town mechanic and high up to the most speculatively inclined capitalist.

If such significant evidence to the contrary fails to persuade those who remain wedded to the notion that the new Constitution was effected by a conspiracy of speculators and counterrevolutionaries, it would seem that the burden of proof rests with the "conspiracy" advocates to offer solid evidence in support of the proposition that the depression was not real but a figment of the imagination, dreamed up by propagandists who sought to scare the simple folk into supporting the move for a stronger federal government. Charles A. Beard sets considerable store by the fact that recovery was under way before the Founding Fathers convened at Philadelphia, and Merrill Jensen finds the period of the Confederation "one of extraordinary economic growth."[46]

Recent economic historians do not find the economic scene quite so healthy, but report a prolonged business depression whose impact was uneven. New England and the Lower South suffered much more than the Middle States, which benefited by prevailing high prices for farm crops. It has been pointed out that our trade with Great Britain, our leading customer, was less in 1790 than it was at the start of the Revolution, although the population of the Thirteen States had expanded in the meantime from 2,500,000 to almost 4,000,000. America was now subject to Britain's restrictive trade measures, excluded from the lucrative British West Indian trade, and liable to all the discriminatory duties leveled against foreign bottoms in our direct trade with other countries. Furthermore, the demand for our staple exports was no longer expanding. Tobacco exports remained stationary, while rice exports actually declined between 1777 and 1791, and the fisheries industry was operating at approximately 80 percent of the prewar level.[47] Even when allowance is made for the shift of America's West Indian trade to the French and Dutch West Indies in this period, the per capita value of all our exports was considerably less in 1790 than prior to the war.[48]

The concept of a prolonged depression is bolstered by the general downturn of commodity prices which took place in the aftermath of peace, with lows established in the years 1788–1789. Significantly, the import price index turned up after 1790, that is, after the inauguration of the new federal government. The fall of prices has been attributed to the outflow of specie and to the behavior of European prices of major export staples. The result, however, was to make the burden of governmental debt heavier, to increase the discontent of the debtor class, and even to contribute in some degree to civil unrest, notably to Shays' Rebellion. Businessmen, mechanics, and artisans witnessed a Confederation government incapable of controlling the money supply, of paying interest on the public debt, or of regulating and encouraging foreign and domestic commerce. Little wonder that these groups recognized the grim necessity for setting up a strong federal government.

Foreign affairs has been a subject consistently neglected by those who regard the government under the Articles as viable. Yet time and again scholars have demonstrated how large was the impact of foreign influence and maritime factors on the domestic issues of the Confederation period. Most recently Julian P. Boyd, in his provocative monograph *Number 7*, has argued, and with much persuasiveness, that the stubborn adherence of the British governmental authorities to mercantilist doctrine in its most orthodox form, their complete repudiation of the free-trade notions advanced by the farsighted if politically inept Earl of Shelburne, may well have contributed "more to the convoking and to the success of the Federal Convention of 1787 than many who sat in that august body." The United States, counting on the dawning of a new economic era, had proffered to Europe a new scheme of commercial reciprocity, but only the Netherlands, Sweden, Prussia, and Morocco had given their virtually meaningless acceptances. Great Britain did not even deign to notice the proffer made in 1786 by John Adams and Thomas Jefferson.

One cannot study the conduct of foreign relations in the Confederation period without being struck at once by the refusal of the Great Powers to deal meaningfully with the United States and by the exaggerated notion propagated by foreign statesmen that the new republic faced inevitable, if not imminent, collapse. In short, it would seem that the investigator might now turn, and with profit, to an evaluation of America's standing and prospects in the community of nations. Such an exploration might well yield at least as much that is pertinent to understanding the causes for summoning the Federal Convention as have the myriad investigations that have measured the stake that debtors or creditors, Eastern townsmen and back-country inhabitants, holders of realty or holders of personality may have had in the establishment of a federal government with effective powers. Indeed, it might prove more relevant than the depth researches which have been undertaken, colony-by-colony, to determine just how widely extended or restricted the voting franchise really was. The fact remains that few Americans challenged the notion that the federal government must have effective control over commerce if the nation was to survive against competition from abroad. Few, if any, denied that only a strong federal government could cope with the problems of national defense, secure the Western lands by forcing the British to quit the frontier posts, acquire from Spain the free navigation of the Mississippi, and end the threats of secession that seemed especially ominous in the trans-Appalachian area.

Since Charles A. Beard's day tons of paper have poured off the presses counting heads, examining pocketbooks, and scrutinizing the motivations of the Founding Fathers. As a result, notably of the researches of Robert E. Brown and Forrest McDonald, it is no longer fashionable to advance the argument that the Constitution was slipped by or put over *undemocratically* in a society that was *undemocratic,* and that a *coup d'état* or conspiracy was effected by substantial holders of personal property as opposed to small farmers and debtors. Slave owners, security holders, and holders of personalty also opposed the Constitution, and the Constitution had among its leading supporters men who did not own a single security. There was, it is true, class feeling and a comprehension of property interest at the time, but by his own words Richard Henry Lee, a leading opponent of the Constitution, minimizes the importance of this conflict.

In a major Antifederalist tract, "Letters from the Federal Farmer,"[49] Lee saw the struggle over the Constitution in part to be a contest over property. "One party," he tells us, "is composed of little insurgents, men in debt, who want no law, and who want a share of the property of others; these are called levelers, Shaysites, etc. The other party is composed of a few, but more dangerous men, with their servile dependents; these avariciously grasp at all power and property." He goes on to stigmatize the latter as "aristocrats, moneyites, etc." who sought to change the form of government because of their "evident dislike to free and equal government." Between these two parties Lee finds "the weight of the community," the men of middling property not in debt, on the one hand, and men, on the other, "content with republican governments, and not aiming at immense fortunes, offices, and powers." In fact, Lee himself concedes that the two extreme parties were "really insignificant, compared with the solid, free, and independent part of the community."

Let us, then, give this notable Antifederalist the last word on this subject. The nature of property holdings did not decide the issue although it could well have influenced individual decisions, nor may the Constitution be put down to a conspiracy by a small faction. Rather was it the result of a national caucus skillfully demonstrating "the art of democratic politics,"[50] specifically, that ability to persuade the "weight of the community," in Lee's words, that a strengthened and vitalized federal system was in the national interest. What was achieved was done within the limits of consensus.

In the last analysis the view that the course of the Confederation period was determined by a counterrevolutionary movement, which, through the instrumentality of the Constitutional Convention, nipped democracy in the bud, hinges upon one's ideas about the American Revolution. Unless one is ready to accept the thesis that the group that started the war were libertarians and democrats and were supplanted by a conservative authoritarian party, one cannot give uncritical adherence to the Smith-Beard-Jensen approach to the Confederation period. The facts simply will not support the argument that the democratic forces originally seized control of the movement in the states. Even in the short run these forces were unsuccessful in every state save Pennsylvania and Georgia. In New Jersey the Constitution, as Mr. McCormick has demonstrated,[51] was welcomed by all classes because it promised needed financial relief. In that state a Western conservative coalition brought about deflationary policies, but not until the very end of the period under review. But the counterrevolution, if the halting of the leftward swing of the pendulum deserves that appellation, was gradual and mild. States like Delaware and Maryland, as John A. Munroe[52] and Philip Crowl[53] have shown us, did not have a counterrevolution, because there never was the kind of democratic upthrust that characterized the early Revolutionary years in Pennsylvania.

The failure of the so-called democratic forces is a tribute to the vigorous Revolutionary leadership of the Whig conservative forces and their awareness of the fundamental issues at stake. It was the Whig conservatives, not the Regulators in North Carolina or the back-country insurgents in Massachusetts, who took the lead in the movement toward independence. Only where the Whig élite seemed timorous and unwilling to move from protest to revolution did the democratic and back-country forces have any chance of seizing power. That was the case in Pennsylvania, where the conservatives had abdicated their political leadership, and to a lesser degree in Georgia, where the story still remains to be spelled out and where the democratic victory was by no means as clear-cut as in Pennsylvania.

The Burke-Bryan-Lee-Clinton forces that comprised the so-called "democratic" party in the Revolutionary years—just what did they stand for? What kind of democracy did they want? The touchstone of their democracy seems to have been an advocacy of a unicameral legislature, a popularly elected judiciary, and a weak executive —and very little else. In some respects the Whig conservatives held more advanced views than did the radicals. Judged by present-day standards the majoritarians were not always liberal. Back-country enthusiasts of the Great Awakening, they were by no means as ready to tolerate non-Protestant religious beliefs as were the deistically minded Whig leaders. In fact, some of the most revealing evidence presented by Mr. Douglass is that which indicates that left-wing Protestants of pietist or evangelical inclinations were fundamentalists in outlook and often basically conservative on political issues. It was they who tried to curb the political rights of non-Protestants, and in Pennsylvania it was the so-called radicals who enacted a law restricting freedom of expression. No, the majoritarians did not always act in democratic ways, nor did they seem always willing to abide by the will of the majority. Witness the shocking abuse of power by the radicals in Pennsylvania who established the state constitution by fiat and did not dare submit it to the people. In fact, they went so far as to require the people to take an oath to support the constitution as a prerequisite to exercising the franchise.

Much has been made of the distrust of the masses held by the Whig conservatives, of the views of men like Jay that "the mass of men are neither wise nor good," although one has no difficulty in citing numerous statements of John Jay expressing faith in the people and in government by consent of the governed. Even if the Whig conservatives did have doubts that the masses were the fountainhead of wisdom, many of the Antifederalists shared their views. Take Samuel Chase, who, as Philip Crowl has shown us, was instrumental in framing Maryland's ultraconservative constitution, and is alleged to have been unstinting in his praise of the aristocratic features of that document, particularly of the electoral college for choosing senators. His desertion to the Antifederalist camp is perhaps best explained by his financial reverses, but he did not linger in it very long. In the federal Convention the Antifederalist John F. Mercer had opposed allowing the people to participate, declaring, "The people cannot know and judge of the characters of Candidates. The worst possible choice will be made."[54] Elbridge Gerry, who refused to sign the Constitution, asserted that "the evils we experience flow from the excess of democracy" and expressed concern at "the danger of the levilling [sic] spirit."[55] In New York the bulwark of Antifederalism was the landowner, with his rural isolation, his dread of the federal impost, and his jealousy of sharing political power. True, he was supported in his opposition to the Constitution by tenants and small farmers, but the Antifederalist leaders of that state had little faith in the people. At the New York Convention George Clinton criticized the people for their fickleness, for their tendency "to vibrate from one extreme to another." It was this very disposition, Clinton confessed, against which he wished to guard.[56]

The Antifederalists were not poured out of one democratic mold;[57] nor did the Federalists represent a unitary point of view about how to strengthen the central government. As Robert East has demonstrated,[58] there was a wide breach between the Bowdoin-Adams kind of federalism in Massachusetts and the Cabot-Pickering stripe of particularism, with its strong sectional and anti-Southern overtones. There was an even wider gulf between the democratic nationalism of Franklin and the authoritarian nationalism of Hamilton.

On the prodemocratic side of the Federalist ledger must be credited the position of the Whig conservatives in support of certain basic human rights which they conceived as fundamental and not subject to change at the caprice of majority rule. Fortunately for the evolution of American democracy, the principles of the conservative revolutionaries and their so-called democratic opponents were largely complementary to each other. Although almost everywhere the radicals were defeated in their efforts to seize the machinery of Revolution, the liberative effects of the war proved a deterrent to the kind of social revolution which would have enshrined class hatreds and ensured violent reaction.

Yes, the American Whigs were divided in the years of the Revolution on almost all issues except that of political independence from Great Britain. Since diverse and even divergent interests forged the Whig alliance, it was only to be expected that the victory of the Patriots would settle no single social or economic issue except freedom from British mercantilist controls, hardly an unmixed blessing in the years of the Confederation. As Harrison Gray Otis once wrote to a friend of Revolutionary days: "You and I did not imagine when the first war with Britain was over that the revolution was just begun."[59]

In terms of the recent past, those who favored increasing the powers of the federal government were more audacious and less tradition-bound than their states' rights opponents. True, nationalists like Robert Morris, John Jay, and Alexander Hamilton might well have preferred a centralized, unitary state,[60] but they were readily persuaded to accept a Constitution which would be more palatable to the masses, one which recognized both the power of the states and the inherent rights of the people. The result, a vitalized federalism and a tightening of the bonds of union, precipitated a greater revolution in American life than did the separation from the mother country. If the adoption of the system of republican federalism constituted a more thoroughgoing break with the political system of the past than did that earlier severing of the tenuous bonds of empire—and there is impressive evidence in the Confederation interlude of our history to substantiate this interpretation—then the Federalists, not the Antifederalists, were the real radicals of their day.

In short, the Revolutionary years, while forming no seamless web, provide far more evidence of continuity than of discontinuity. It is perhaps not purely fortuitous that only a handful of the forty-three living Signers of the Declaration of Independence expressed any vocal opposition to the Constitution, while a full thirty openly worked for its adoption. The Signers' endorsement gives special weight to the later observation of John Quincy Adams that the Great Declaration and the Constitution were parts of "one consistent whole," a logical sequence of a continuous effort by which foundations were laid for a government resting on reason and consent.[61] Neither the Constitutional Convention nor the ratifying conventions provide evidence of any counterrevolution. Rather they show how the Founding Fathers, by demonstrating their skill in the art of democratic politics, were able to fashion a national reform caucus.[62]

Above all, the Constitutional period is a continuation of the Revolutionary Age. The ratifying conventions proved revolutionary instruments of the people in the same sense

that the ratifying convention that adopted the Massachusetts Constitution of 1780 was a novel revolutionary
mechanism for registering the consent of the governed in
establishing a new fundamental charter. The War of the
Revolution heralded the end of parochial colonialism and
the fulfillment of nationhood; the Constitution, which
underwrote national survival, must be considered an integral step in that revolutionary process. Triggered by
the pressures for decolonization, the American Revolution
quickly burgeoned into a broader movement of national
self-determination, constitutional re-creation, and social
and intellectual liberation. And in that more expanded
sense the Revolution is as integral a part of the Nuclear
Space Age, with its global preoccupations, as it was of the
more circumscribed, if no less heroic, Age of Washington.

NOTES TO CHAPTER IV

1. Merrill Jensen, who expounded this view in *The Articles
of Confederation* (reprint with new foreword, Madison, Wis.,
1948), has more recently modified his stand and suggested that
the Articles were, "in a negative sense at least, a democratic
government." "Democracy and the American Revolution,"
Huntington Library Quarterly, XX (1957), 339.

2. For examples from New England, see Lee N. Newcomber,
*The Embattled Farmers: A Massachusetts Countryside in the
American Revolution* (New York, 1953); Oscar Zeichner,
Connecticut's Years of Controversy, 1750–1776 (Chapel Hill,
1949).

3. See Chilton Williamson, *American Suffrage from Property to Democracy, 1760–1860* (Princeton, 1960); Robert E.
Brown, *Middle-Class Democracy and the Revolution in Massachusetts, 1691–1780* (Ithaca, N.Y., 1955).

4. Estimates range from 68 percent, according to Roger
Champagne, to 90 percent of the adult white males, according
to Milton M. Klein. Cf. Roger Champagne, "Family Politics vs.
Constitutional Principles: the New York Assembly Elections of
1768 and 1769," *William and Mary Quarterly* (January, 1963);

Milton M. Klein, "Politics and Personalities in Colonial New York," *New York History* (1966), p. 10; Bernard Friedman, "The New York Assembly Elections of 1768 and 1769: The Disruption of Family Politics," *loc. cit.* (January, 1965).

5. See H. L. Morais, "The Sons of Liberty in New York," in R. B. Morris, ed., *The Era of the American Revolution* (New York, 1939), pp. 269–289.

6. See Roger J. Champagne, "The Sons of Liberty and the Aristocracy in New York Politics" (Ph.D. thesis, Univ. of Wisconsin, 1960); L. Jesse Lemish, "Jack Tar vs. John Bull: The Role of New York's Seamen in Precipitating the Revolution" (Ph.D. thesis, Yale University, 1962). For the lack of resistance to mobbism in America as compared with contemporary England and France, see Gordon S. Wood, "A Note on Mobs in the American Revolution," *William and Mary Quarterly*, XXIII (1966), 635–642.

7. Thomas Hutchinson, *The History of the Colony and Province of Massachusetts-Bay,* ed. by L. S. Mayo (Cambridge, Mass., 1936), III, 135, 136.

8. See Staughton Lynd and Alfred Young, "Carl Becker: The Mechanics and New York City Politics, 1774–1801," *Labor History,* V (1964), 215 *et seq.*

9. For the Charleston Mechanics, see Richard Walsh, *Charleston's Sons of Liberty: A Study of the Artisans, 1763–1789* (Columbia, S.C., 1959).

10. *The Writings of George Washington from the Original Manuscript Sources, 1745–1799,* ed. J. C. Fitzpatrick (Washington, 1931–1944), XXVIII, 502; XXIX, 27, 34.

11. *Ibid.,* XXIX, 51.

12. Henry Lee to George Washington, Oct. 17, 1786, *Letters of Members of the Continental Congress,* ed. E. C. Burnett (Washington, 1921–1933), VIII, 486.

13. *The Papers of Thomas Jefferson,* ed. Julian P. Boyd (Princeton, 1950), X, 574.

14. *Ibid.,* p. 489.

15. *The Writings of George Washington . . . ,* ed. Jared Sparks (Boston, 1834–1837), IX, 243 n.

16. *Records of the Federal Convention of 1787,* ed. Max Farrand (New Haven, 1911–1937), I, 19, 24, 25.

17. See especially *Federalist*, 1, 15, 16, and 85.

18. Adams to Jay, June 26, 1785, *Works of John Adams*, ed. C. F. Adams (Boston, 1850–1856), VIII, 276.

19. *Advertiser*, New York, July 21, 1787.

20. Jefferson to Madison, July 1, 1784, *Jefferson Papers*, VII, 356.

21. *Jefferson Papers*, X, 14 ff. Similarly, John Jay to Matthew Ridley, March 31, 1785—Massachusetts Historical Society.

22. *Complete Works of Benjamin Franklin*, ed. John Bigelow (New York, 1887–1888), IX, 300–301.

23. Freeman H. Hart, *The Valley of Virginia in the American Revolution* (Chapel Hill, 1942), pp. 123–125. For evidence from the court records of sharply mounting indebtedness in central and western Massachusetts, see R. B. Morris, "Insurrection in Massachusetts," in *America in Crisis*, ed. Daniel Aaron (New York, 1952), p. 24. On the steady upsurge of insolvency in Connecticut during the entire Confederation period, see *Public Records of the State of Connecticut* (1776–1796), eds. C. J. Hoadly and L. W. Labaree (Hartford, 1894–1951), VII, xv, xvi.

24. R. R. Livingston Papers, Bancroft Transcripts, New York Public Library.

25. *Compilation of the Messages and Papers of the Presidents, 1789–1902*, ed. J. D. Richardson (Washington, 1903), II, 643.

26. George Ticknor Curtis, *History of the Origin, Formation, and Adoption of the Constitution of the United States* . . . (New York, 1854), I, xi, 233, 234, 330.

27. George Bancroft, *History of the Formation of the Constitution of the United States of America* (New York, 1885), I, 262–266. For Bancroft's temperate treatment of Shays' Rebellion, see, *ibid.*, pp. 274–275; cf. Richard Hildreth, *The History of the United States of America* (New York, 1848–1851), III, 472–477.

28. William Henry Trescot, *The Diplomatic History of the Administrations of Washington and Adams: 1789–1801* (Boston, 1857), p. 9. Long before Trescot, however, Richard Henry Lee, a leading Antifederalist, wrote, Oct. 8, 1787: "I know our situation is critical, and it behoves us to make the

best of it." "Letters of the Federal Farmer," Letter I, in *Pamphlets on the Constitution of the United States,* ed. P. L. Ford (Brooklyn, 1888), p. 280.

29. Richard Frothingham, *The Rise of the Republic of the United States* (Boston, 1910; first published in 1872), pp. 583 ff.; James Schouler, *History of the United States of America under the Constitution* (revised ed., New York, 1894), I, 13 ff.; H. von Holst, *The Constitutional and Political History of the United States,* trans. John J. Lalor and Alfred B. Mason (Chicago, 1889–1892), I, 37.

30. John Fiske, *The Critical Period of American History, 1783–1789* (Boston and New York, 1888), pp. 55–57, and Chap. IV, *passim.*

31. John Bach McMaster, *A History of the People of the United States, From the Revolution to the Civil War* (New York, 1883–1913), I, 313.

32. Andrew C. McLaughlin, *The Confederation and the Constitution, 1783–1789* (New York and London, 1905), pp. 71, 107, 156, 161. For McLaughlin's low estimate of Fiske's scholarship, see *ibid.,* pp. 319–320.

33. Henry B. Dawson, "The Motley Letter," *Historical Magazine,* 2nd Ser., IX (March, 1871), 157 ff.

34. J. Allen Smith, *The Spirit of American Government: A Study of the Constitution, Its Origin, Influence, and Relation to Democracy* (Chautauqua, 1911), p. 37.

35. Charles A. Beard, *An Economic Interpretation of the Constitution of the United States* (New York, 1949), pp. 3–4.

36. *Ibid.,* pp. 47–48.

37. Charles A. Beard and Mary R. Beard, *The Rise of American Civilization* (New York, 1930; first published in 1927), I, 326.

38. Beard, *The Enduring Federalist* (New York, 1948), pp. 27–30.

39. *The Articles of Confederation: An Interpretation of the Social-Constitutional History of the American Revolution, 1774–1781* (University of Wisconsin, 1940; second printing with additional foreword, 1948). *The New Nation: A History of the United States During the Confederation, 1781–1789* (New York, 1950).

40. E. J. Ferguson, "State Assumption of Federal Debt

During the Confederation," *Mississippi Valley Historical Rev.*, XXXVIII (1951), 403.

41. Allan Nevins, *The American States During and After the American Revolution* (New York, 1927), p. 541.

42. Forrest McDonald, *E Pluribus Unum* (Boston, 1965).

43. Samuel Adams to Samuel Cooper, Nov. 7, 1780; James Warren to Samuel Adams, Dec. 4, 1780; Connecticut Delegates to the Governor of Connecticut, Jan. 16, 1781. Burnett, *Letters of Members of the Continental Congress,* V, 440, 488 n., 536–537.

44. Robert Morris to John Jay, July 13, 1781. Wharton, *Diplomatic Correspondence of the American Revolution,* IV, 563; Jay Papers, Columbia University Library.

45. Morris to President of Congress, Feb. 26, 1783. Wharton, *Rev. Dip. Corr.,* VI, 266; *Journals of the Continental Congress,* XXIV, 151.

46. Merrill Jensen, *The New Nation* (New York, 1950), pp. 423–424.

47. Timothy Pitkin, *A Statistical View of the Commerce of the United States of America* (New Haven, 1935), pp. 84–85.

48. See Curtis P. Nettels, *The Emergence of a National Economy, 1775–1815* (New York, 1962); Douglass C. North, *The Economic Growth of the United States, 1790–1860* (New York, 1961), pp. 18, 19; Gordon C. Bjork, "The Weaning of the American Economy," *Journal of Economic History,* XXIV (1964), 541–560.

49. *Pamphlets on the Constitution,* ed. by Paul L. Ford (1888).

50. See John P. Roche, "The Founding Fathers: A Reform Caucus in Action," *American Political Science Rev.,* LV (1961), 799.

51. Richard P. McCormick, *Experiment in Independence: New Jersey in the Critical Period, 1781–1789* (New Brunswick, 1950).

52. *Federalist Delaware, 1775–1815* (New Brunswick, 1954).

53. *Maryland During and After the Revolution* (Baltimore, 1942).

54. *Records of the Federal Convention of 1787,* ed. Max Farrand (New Haven, 1911–1937) II, 205.

55. *Ibid.*, I, 48.

56. *Debates in the Several State Conventions on the Adoption of the Federal Constitution . . . Together with the Journal of the Federal Convention . . .*, ed. Jonathan Elliot (Philadelphia, 1881), II, 359.

57. The reader is referred to the provocative article by Cecelia M. Kenyon, "Men of Little Faith: The Anti-Federalists on the Nature of Representative Government," *William and Mary Quarterly*, 3rd Ser., XII (1955), 3–43.

58. "The Massachusetts Conservatives in the Critical Period," in *The Era of the American Revolution*, ed. R. B. Morris (New York, 1939), pp. 349–391.

59. Samuel Eliot Morison, *The Life and Letters of Harrison Gray Otis* (Boston and New York, 1913), I, 49.

60. W. W. Crosskey, *Politics and the Constitution* (2 vols., Chicago, 1953), argues that the Constitution was in fact designed to create such a centralized state, but his evidence, while diffuse, is far from persuasive.

61. J. Q. Adams, *Jubilee of the Constitution: A Discourse Delivered at the Request of the New York Historical Society, April 30, 1839* (New York, 1839), pp. 40–41.

62. See John P. Roche, "The Founding Fathers: A Reform Caucus in Action," *American Political Science Rev.*, LV (1961), 799–816. There was, indubitably, an increase in the number of middling class, yeoman, and artisan representatives in the state legislatures after the war. Such evidence, however, points to growing egalitarianism rather than to counterrevolution. See J. T. Main, "Government by the People: The American Revolution and the Democratization of the Legislatures," *William and Mary Quarterly*, XXIII (1966), 391–407.

Index

Aaron, Daniel, 164n
Adams, John, 9, 24, 67, 107, 160; and Boston Massacre Trial, 9–11; on American Revolution, 14, 15, 17, 35; denies Parliament's legislative authority, 36–37; on Spain, 55; and collection of Virginia debts, 82–83; publication of papers, 95; opposes foreign military alliances, 97; told of plans to divide America, 113; opposes truce, 116–117; on weakness of Articles of Confederation, 138; supports Constitution, 148; offers plan for commercial reciprocity, 154–155
Adams, John Quincy, 94, 161
Adams, Samuel, ix, 10, 46, 148, 150
Adams Legal Papers, 9
Alamance, 70
Albany, 59
Alexander, William, Lord Stirling, 65
Allen, Ethan, 11, 54
American Civil War, 4, 5
American Revolution, relevance today, x, 1–6; compared to French, 2, 35, 44–52, 54, 77; as anticolonial war, 3, 84; portrait of, 6, 7, 14; as New England conspiracy, 17–19; as struggle over sovereignty, 35; interest groups in, 36; consensus and continuity in, 44–45; common origins with French, 46, 48, 49, 50; as conservative force, 51; class consciousness in, 54–69; class structure and, 55; as civil war, 68–69; contrasted to French Terror, 69; hardships of, 69; the Negro in, 71–75; as social revolution, 77; confiscation in, 77–79; cancelling of debts in, 81–83; as reform movement, 83–85; dual character of, 85; romantic notions of,

92; diplomacy of, 93–125; as war for home rule and internal struggle, 128–134; Constitution as climax of, 135, 152, 157–162
Andrews, Charles M., 26, 89n
Andrews, Evangeline, 89n
Annapolis, 78
Antifederalism, 134, 137
Antifederalists, 129, 133, 136, 146, 147, 148, 156–157, 160, 161; School of historians, 128–129, 136, 142; view of masses, 159
Aranjuez, summer home of Spanish royal family, 39; secret pact of, 105
Arendt, Hannah, 2, 48
Articles of Confederation, 117, 128, 135; J. Allen Smith on, 143; Merrill Jensen on, 146; as reflection of States'-rights temper, 149; weakness of Congress under, 150
Auckland Manuscripts, 94

Babeuf, François Émile, French revolutionist, 50, 51, 52
Bailyn, Bernard, 37, 38
Bancroft, Dr. Edward, double agent, 12, 13, 94, 98, 120
Bancroft, George, historian, 22–25, 57, 136, 141, 145, 164n
Bank of North America, 150
Barbé-Marbois, François, 53, 94, 120
Barré, Isaac, 20
Beard, Charles A., 136, 153, 155, 157; interpretation of Constitution, 144–147
Becker, Carl Lotus, historian, 128, 129, 134
Beckwith, George, 106
Bedford, Gunning, 138
Bedford, John Russell, 4th Duke of, 58
Beer, George Louis, historian, 26, 27

taxing power to Congress, 152;
Antifederalists in, 159
New York City, 11, 45, 48, 70,
111, 129, 133; distribution of
Loyalist property in, 78; property
qualifications in, 131; working
classes of, 132; lawlessness in,
143
Nicholas, Robert Carter, 74
Nonimportation, 59
North, Frederick, Lord North, First
Lord of the Treasury, 32, 110
North Carolina, regulator move-
ment in, 60, 69, 70, 71, 129,
158
North ministry, 28, 50, 76; ap-
proves "New Ireland" plan, 63;
overthrow prevented, 104–105;
and Cumberland-Floridablanca
negotiations, 108
North Vietnam, 134
Nova Scotia, 63
Nuclear Age, 3, 162

Oldmixon, John, 26
Oliver, Peter, 1, 16, 17
Oriente, Congo, 123
Osborn, Sir Danvers, Governor of
N.Y., 19
Osgood, Herbert L., 26
Oswald, Richard, 112, 113, 122
Otis, Harrison Gray, 160
Otis, James, Sir., 17
Otis, James, Jr., 47, 49; and Writs
of Assistance, 17, 18; and Town-
shend Acts, 21; on the mob, 67

Paine, Thomas, x, 35, 50, 97, 141,
142
Palmer, Robert R., 41, 129
Panin, Nikita Ivanovitch, Count,
and peace mediations, 114, 115,
117
Papers of the Continental Congress,
95
Paris, 9, 45, 125
Parrington, Vernon, 145
Patronage, 29, 30
Patroons, 57
Peace Commissioners, 34, 64, 106;
papers of, 95; distinctive style of,
125

Pepperell, Sir William, 65
Penn, Lady Juliana, 79
Penn, William, estates of, 49
Pennsylvania, 157; ratifying con-
vention of, 138; conservative ma-
jority in legislature, 150; restric-
tion of freedoms in, 158
Pershing, General John Joseph, 93
Peters, Richard, 151
Peters, Reverend Samuel, 66
Philadelphia, 26, 129, 140, 149,
153
Pickering, Timothy, 160
Place de la Bastille, 45
Place de la Concorde, 45
Place de la République, 45
Plymouth, 16
Population, of colonies, 15
Postlethwayt, Malachy, 15
Presbyterians, 131
Preston, Captain Thomas, 9, 10
Primogeniture, 55; abolition of, 79–
81
Proclamation against Nullification,
140
Providence, 132
Prussia, 154
Pulteney, Sir William, 113
Puritanism, 38

Quai d'Orsay, diplomatic docu-
ments in, 94, 120
Quebec Act of 1774, 24
Quincy, Josiah, Jr., 10
Quitrent, 55, 61

Ramsay, David, historian, 17, 23,
37, 38
Randolph, Edmund, 137
Rayneval, Joseph-Matthias Gérard
de, 116; secret peace mission to
England, 113, 121, 122; opposes
American claims to West, 118
Real Property Act, 81
Reciprocity, 154–155; in Treaty ne-
gotiations, 34–35
Regulator Movement. *See* North
Carolina
Reuther, Walter, 45
Revolution of 1688, 39